FIRST 50 KIDS' SONGS

YOU SHOULD PLAY ON THE PIANO

ISBN 978-1-4950-7453-0

HAL•LEONARD®

7777 W. BLUEMOUND RD. P.O. BOX 13819 MILWAUKEE, WI 53213

Visit Hal Leonard Online at
www.halleonard.com

ADDAMS FAMILY THEME

Theme from the TV Show and Movie

Music and Lyrics by
VIC MIZZY

Moderately

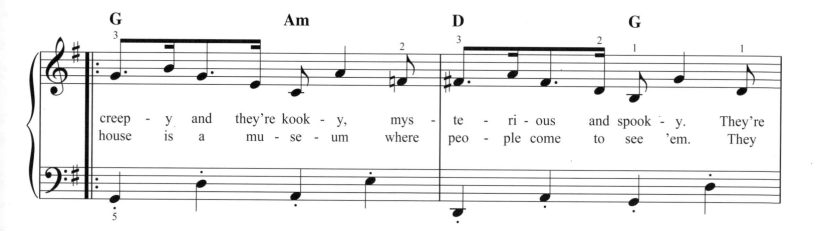

creep - y and they're kook - y, mys - te - ri - ous and spook - y. They're
house is a mu - se - um where peo - ple come to see 'em. They

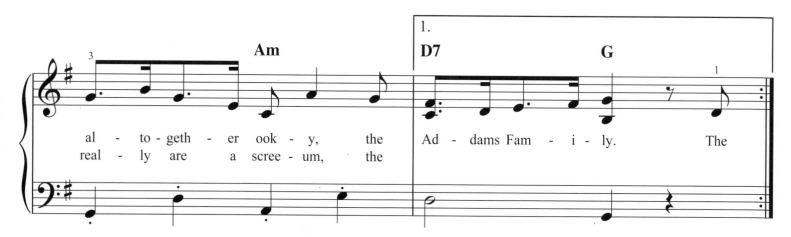

al - to - geth - er ook - y, the Ad - dams Fam - i - ly. The
real - ly are a scree - um, the

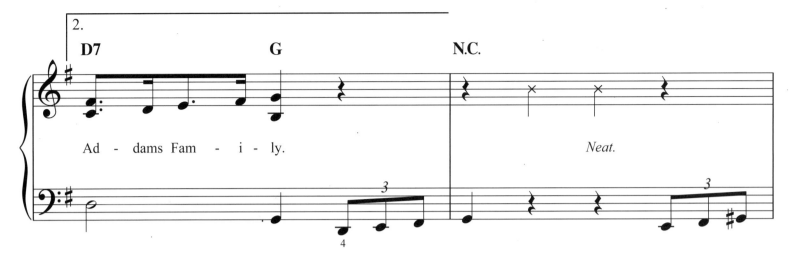

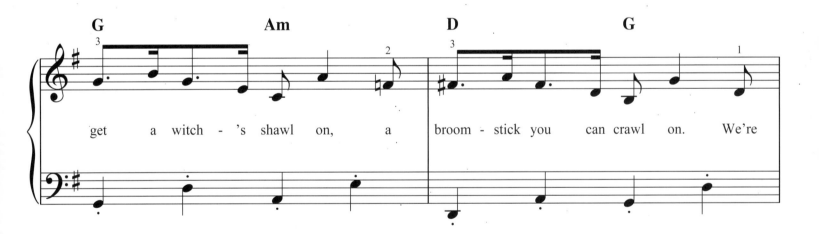

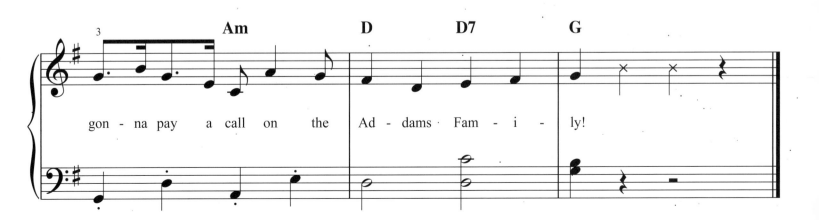

ALPHABET SONG

Traditional

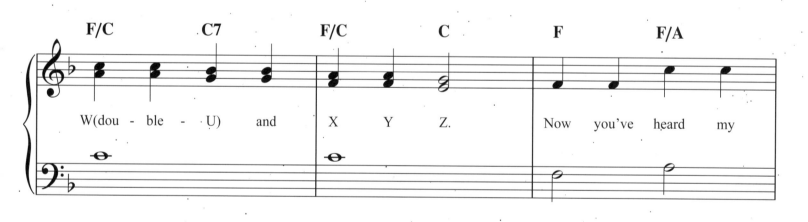

"C" IS FOR COOKIE
from the Television Series SESAME STREET

Words and Music by
JOE RAPOSO

With a jiggle and a bounce

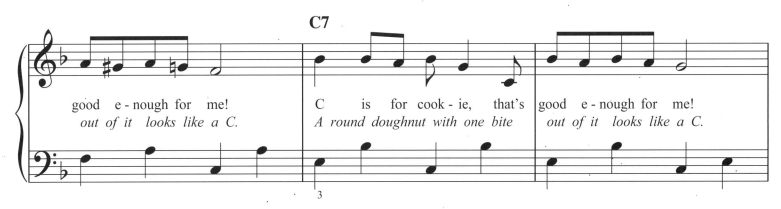

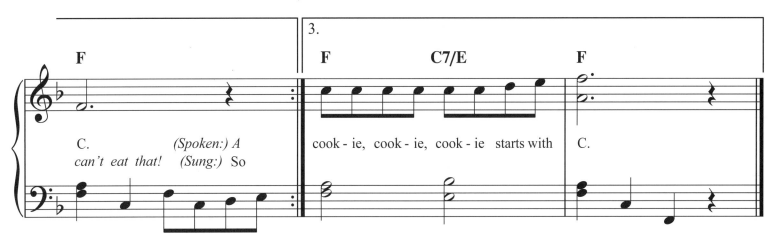

ANY DREAM WILL DO

from JOSEPH AND THE AMAZING TECHNICOLOR® DREAMCOAT

Music by ANDREW LLOYD WEBBER
Lyrics by TIM RICE

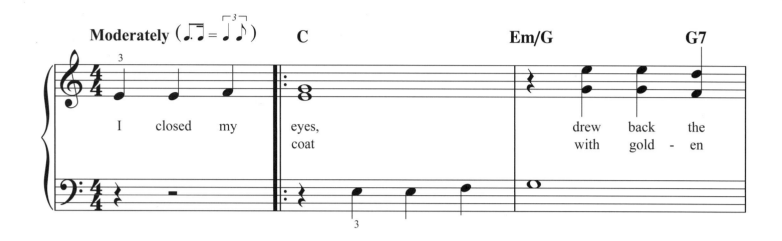

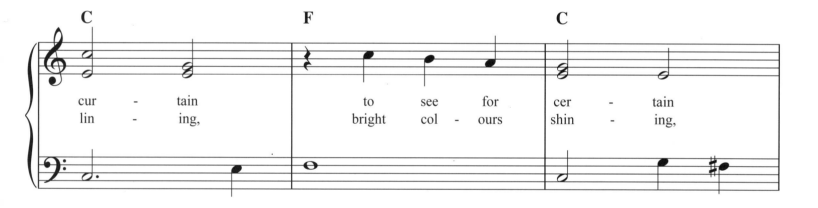

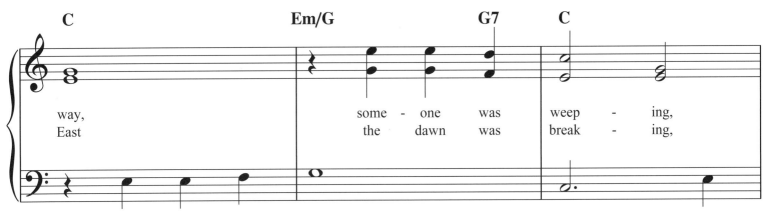

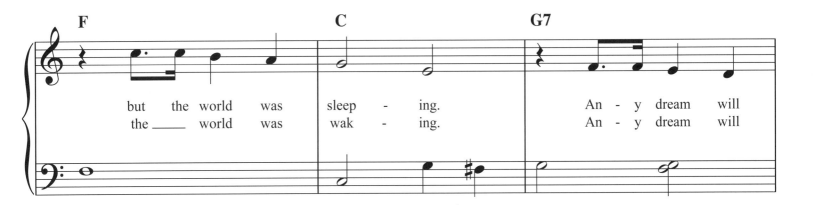

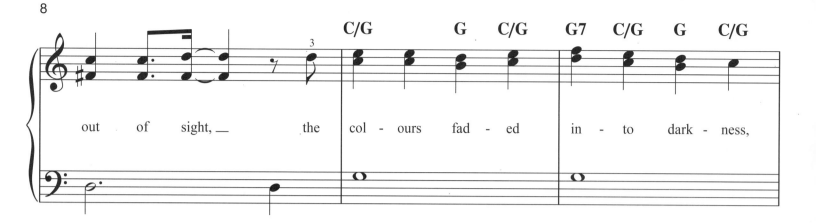

out of sight, ___ the col - ours fad - ed in - to dark - ness,

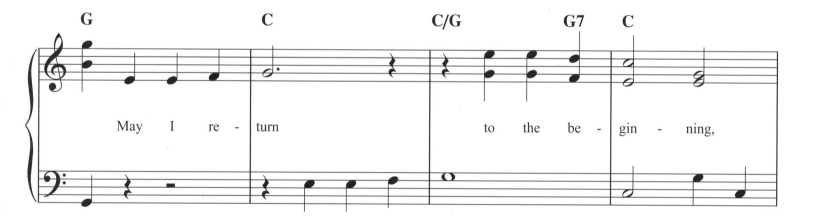

I was left a - lone.

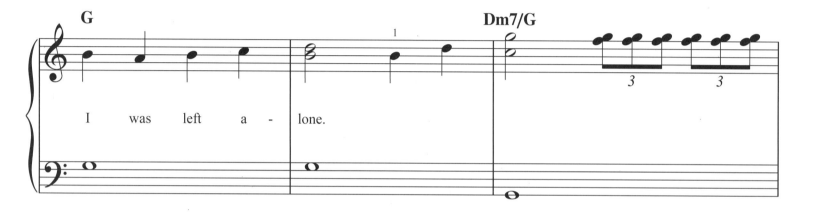

May I re - turn to the be - gin - ning,

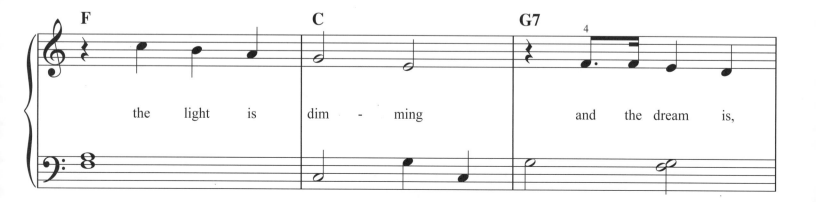

the light is dim - ming and the dream is,

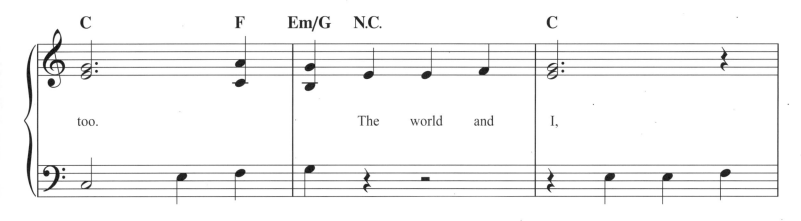

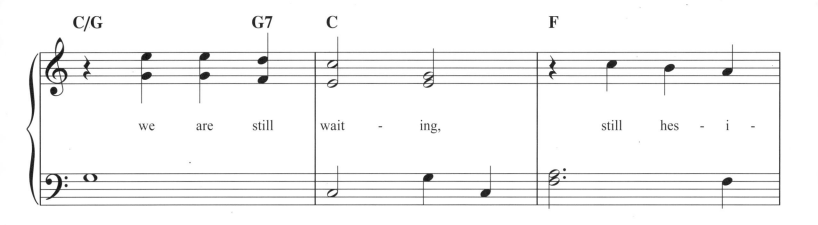

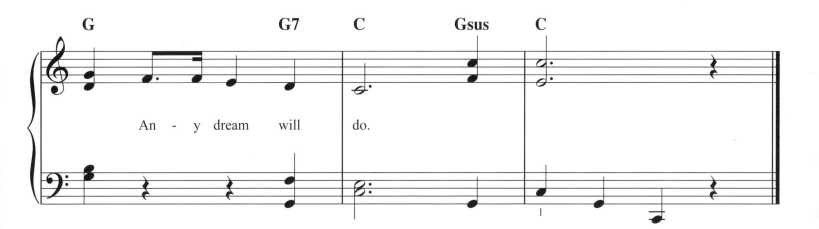

BANANAS IN PYJAMAS

Words and Music by
CAREY BLYTON

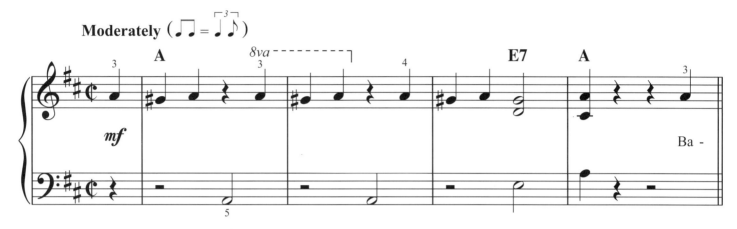

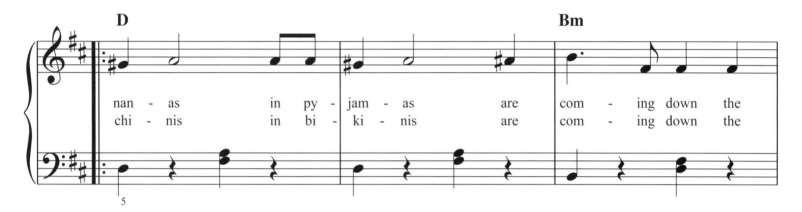

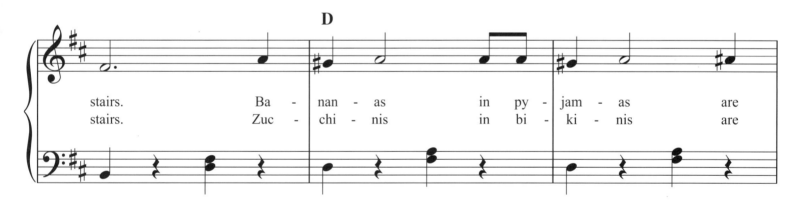

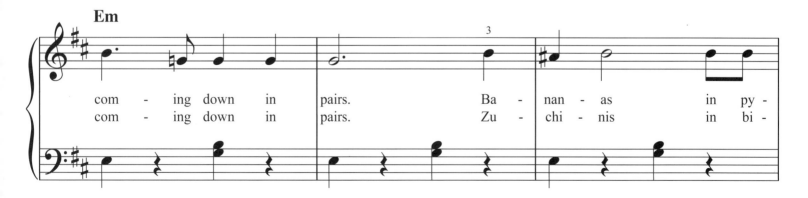

jam - as   are   chas - ing ted - dy   bears,   'cos   on Tues - days
ki - nis   are   chas - ing ted - dy   bears,   'cos   on Tues - days

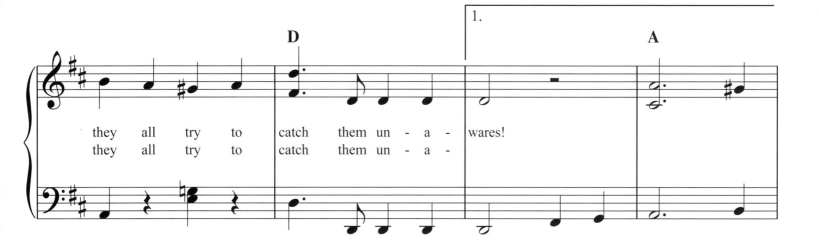

they   all   try   to   catch   them un - a - wares!
they   all   try   to   catch   them un - a -

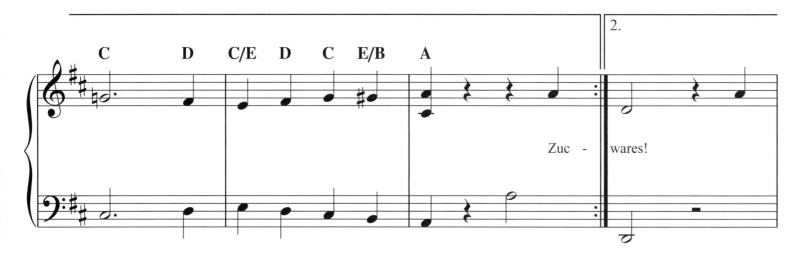

Zuc - wares!

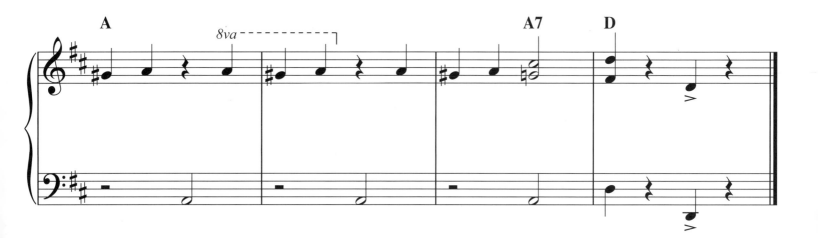

THE CANDY MAN

from WILLY WONKA AND THE CHOCOLATE FACTORY

Words and Music by LESLIE BRICUSSE
and ANTHONY NEWLEY

Freely, but not too slowly

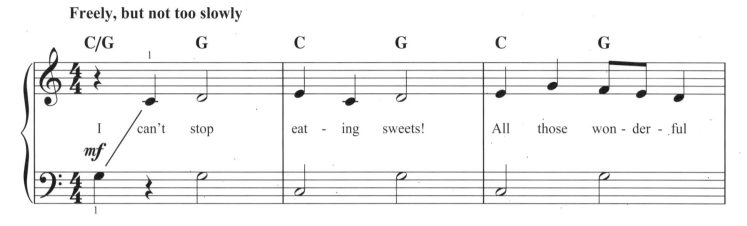

I / can't stop   eat - ing sweets!   All   those won - der - ful

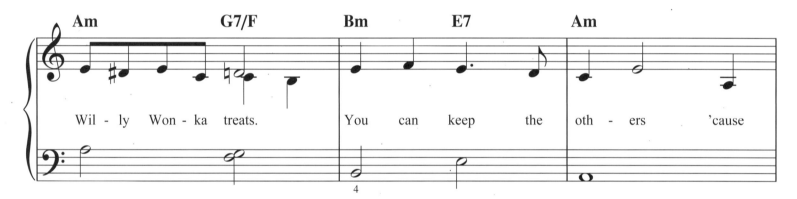

Wil - ly Won - ka treats.   You   can   keep   the   oth - ers   'cause

me,   I'm   a   Won - ker - er.   When   it   comes   to

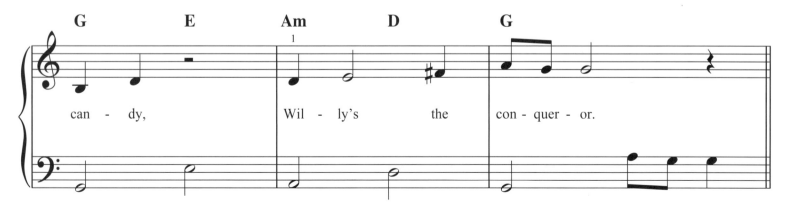

can - dy,   Wil - ly's   the   con - quer - or.

Easy Swing, joyously ($\sqrt{}$ = $\sqrt{}$)

C

Who can take a sun - rise, _____
Who can take a rain - bow, _____
Who can take tom - mor - row, _____

Dm   **G**

sprin - kle it with dew, _____
wrap it in a sigh, _____
dip it in a dream, _____

Fmaj7   **B♭7/D**   **C**   **Am7**

cov - er it with choc - 'late and a mir - a - cle or two?
soak it in the sun and make a straw - b'ry lem - on pie?   The
sep - a - rate the sor - row and col - lect up all the cream?

Am/D   **D7/F♯**   **Dm7/F**   **C**   **F**

can - dy man, _____   the can - dy man can,

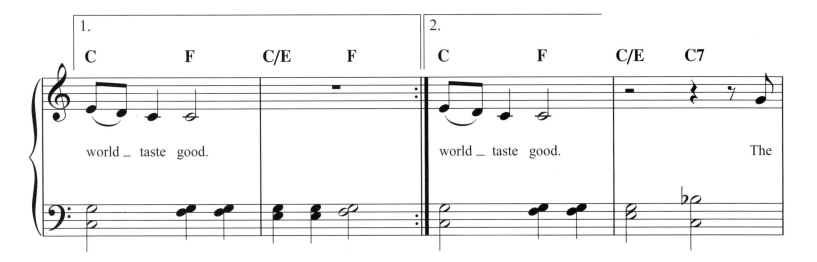

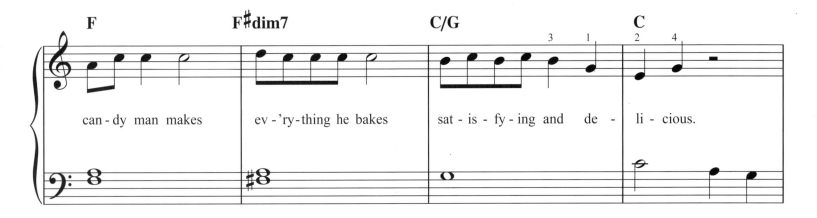

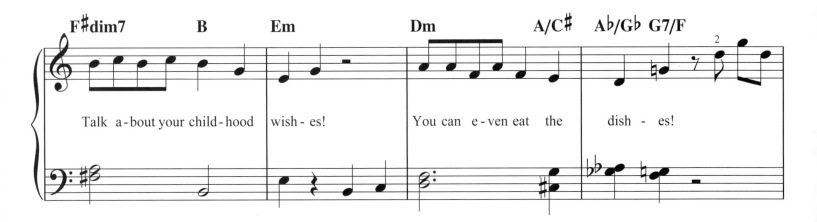

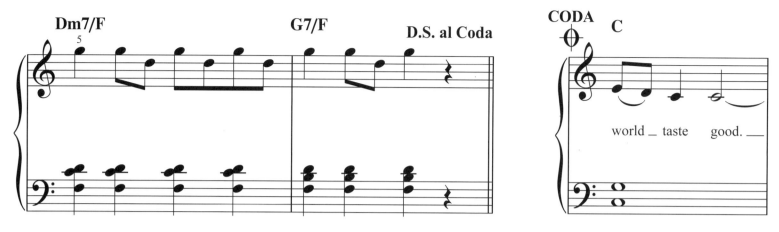

THE CHICKEN DANCE

By TERRY RENDALL
and WERNER THOMAS
English Lyrics by PAUL PARNES

Do you wan-na feel good, wan-na laugh and

play? (Let's laugh and play.) Wan-na have some fun,

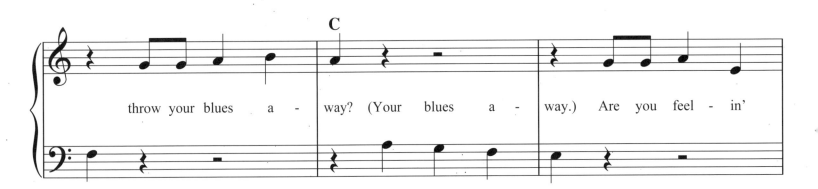

throw your blues a - way? (Your blues a - way.) Are you feel-in'

sad? Got a prob-lem? Here's a cure. (We got the

To Coda ⊕

cure.)   Do   the   chick - en   dance;   make   you   hap - py   for

sure. _____   Reach   out   your   arms   and

swing   your   part - ner.   Make   like   a

bird   and   try   to   fly.

Come on out there, you hens and

roost - er. Just hook your arms now,

D.S. al Coda

and don't be shy.___ Do you wan - na feel

CODA

sure. ___

CHITTY CHITTY BANG BANG

from CHITTY CHITTY BANG BANG

Words and Music by RICHARD M. SHERMAN
and ROBERT B. SHERMAN

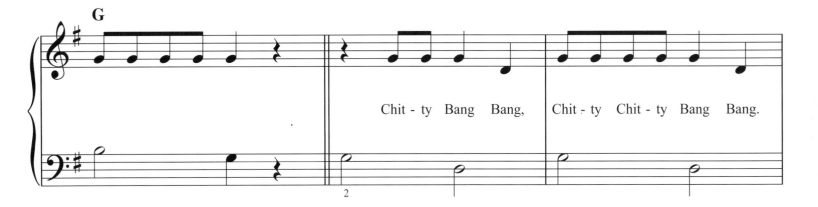

Chit - ty Bang Bang, Chit - ty Chit - ty Bang Bang.

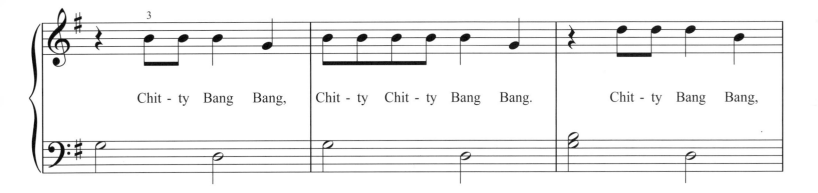

Chit - ty Bang Bang, Chit - ty Chit - ty Bang Bang. Chit - ty Bang Bang,

Chit - ty Chit - ty Bang Bang! Oh, you, pret - ty Chit - ty Bang Bang,

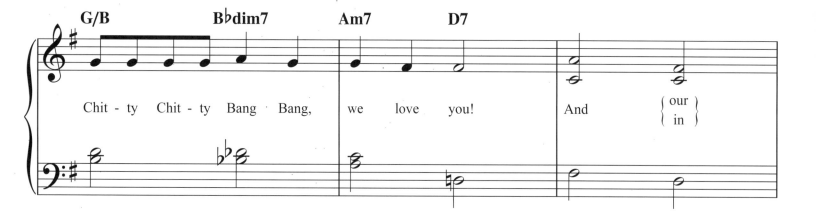

G/B **B♭dim7** **Am7** **D7**

Chit - ty Chit - ty Bang Bang, we love you! And { our } { in }

D **Am** **G**

pret - ty Chit - ty Bang Bang, Chit - ty Chit - ty Bang Bang, { loves us too! } { what we'll do! }

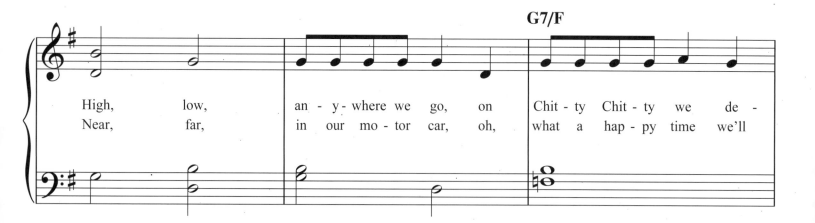

G7/F

High, low, an - y-where we go, on Chit - ty Chit - ty we de -
Near, far, in our mo - tor car, oh, what a hap - py time we'll

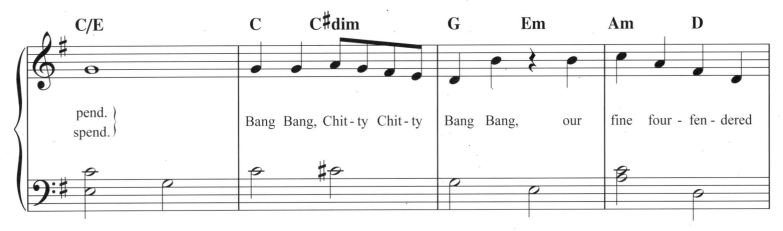

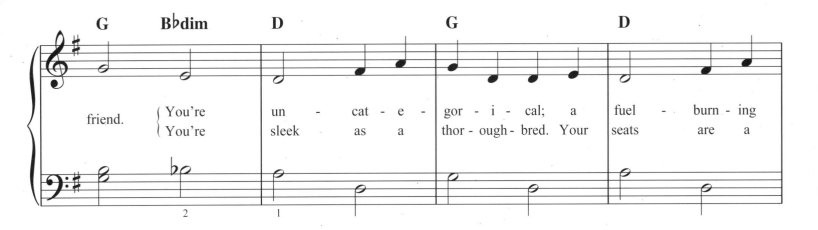

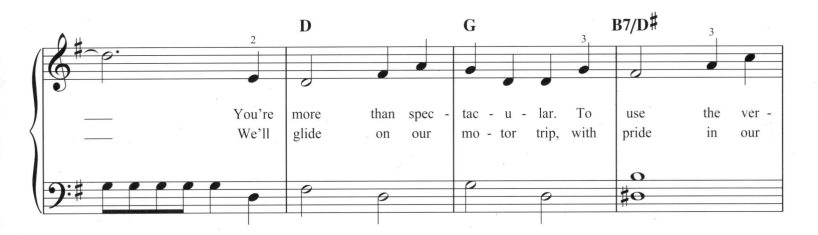

nac - u - lar, you're | wiz - ard! You're | smash - ing! You're | keen! _____
own - er - ship, the | en - vy of | all we sur - | vey! _____

Oh, Chit-ty, you, Chit-ty, | pret-ty Chit-ty Bang Bang. | Chit-ty Chit-ty Bang Bang,

we love you! | And Chit-ty, {our/in} Chit-ty, | pret-ty Chit-ty Bang Bang, | Chit-ty Chit-ty Bang Bang,

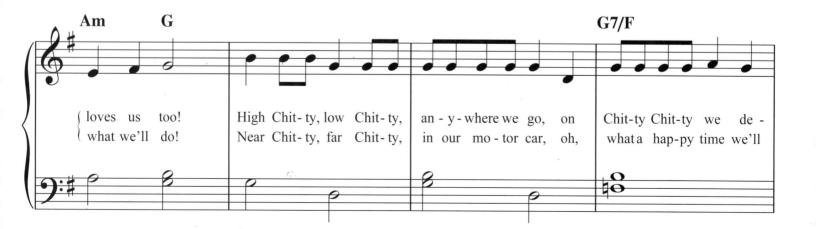

{loves us too!/what we'll do!} | High Chit-ty, low Chit-ty, | an - y-where we go, on | Chit-ty Chit-ty we de -
Near Chit-ty, far Chit-ty, | in our mo-tor car, oh, | what a hap-py time we'll

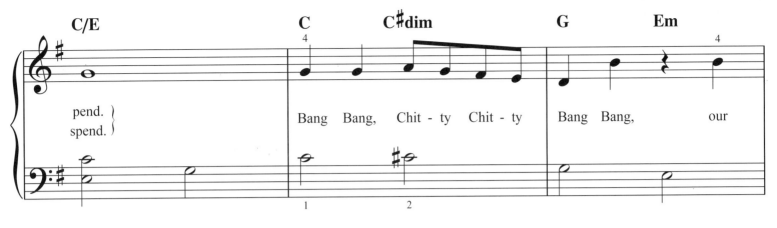

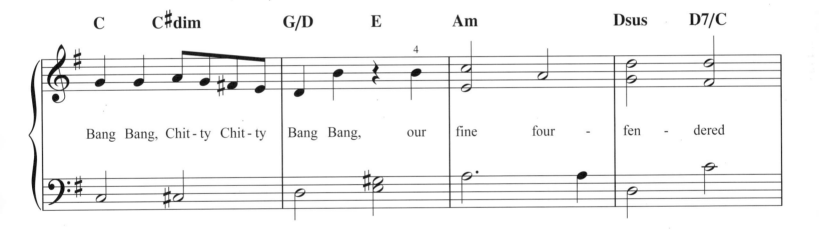

DING-DONG! THE WITCH IS DEAD

from THE WIZARD OF OZ

Lyrics by E.Y. "YIP" HARBURG
Music by HAROLD ARLEN

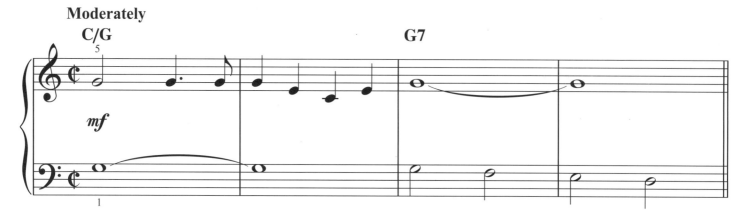

Once there was a wick-ed witch in the love-ly land of Oz, and a

wick-ed-er, wick-ed-er, wick-ed-er witch there nev-er, nev-er was. She

filled the folks in Munch-kin-land with ter-ror and with dread, 'til

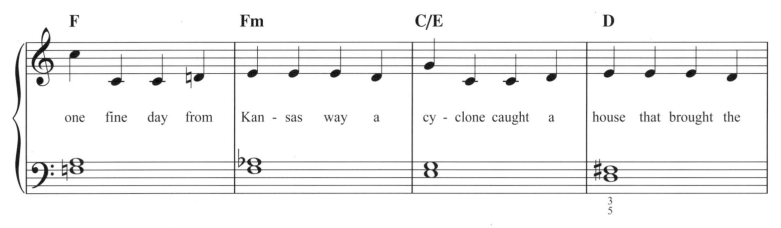

one fine day from Kan - sas way a cy - clone caught a house that brought the

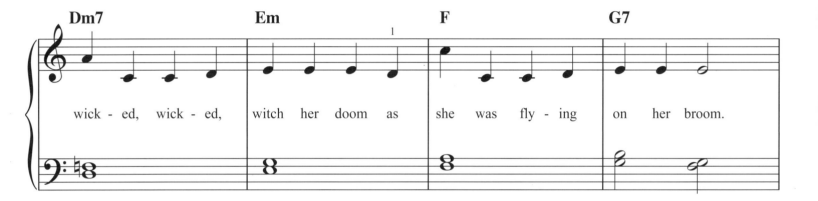

wick - ed, wick - ed, witch her doom as she was fly - ing on her broom.

For the house fell on her head and the

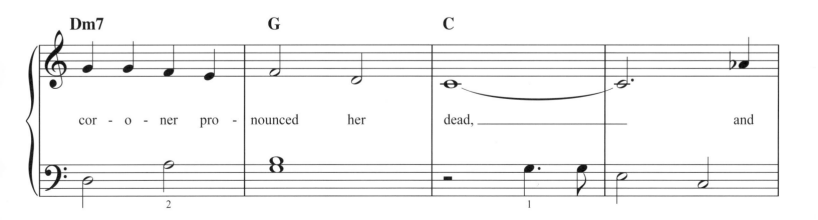

cor - o - ner pro - nounced her dead, _____ and

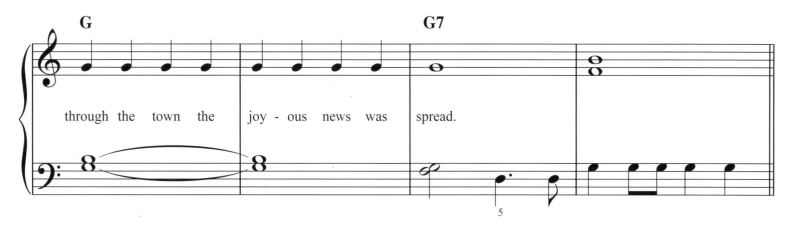

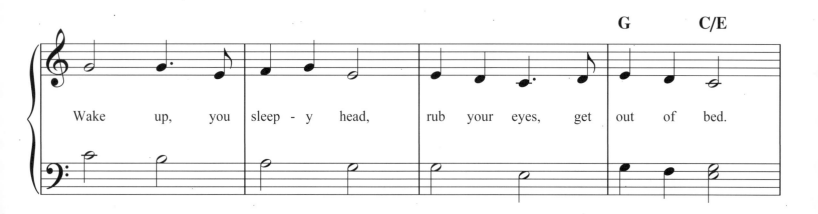

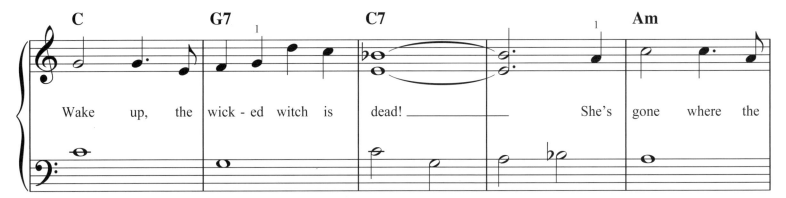

C　　　　**G7**　　　　**C7**　　　　　　　　**Am**

Wake up, the wick-ed witch is dead! _____ She's gone where the

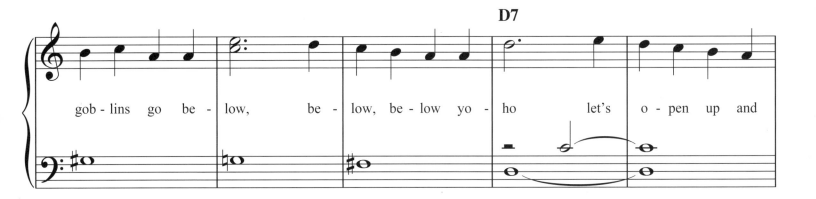

　　　　　　　　　　　　　　　　D7

gob-lins go be-low, be-low, be-low yo-ho let's o-pen up and

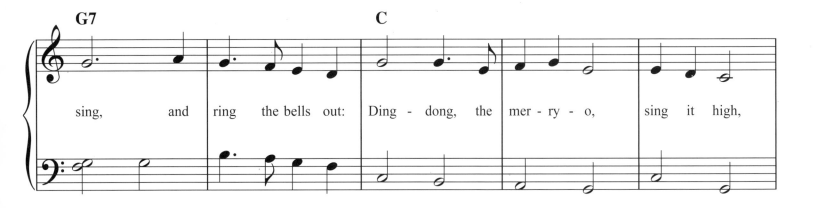

G7　　　　　　　　**C**

sing, and ring the bells out: Ding-dong, the mer-ry-o, sing it high,

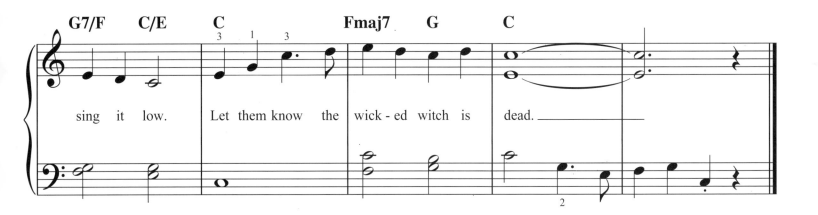

G7/F　　**C/E**　　**C**　　　**Fmaj7**　　**G**　　**C**

sing it low. Let them know the wick-ed witch is dead. _____

DITES-MOI
(Tell Me Why)
from SOUTH PACIFIC

Lyrics by OSCAR HAMMERSTEIN II
Music by RICHARD RODGERS

Moderately

Di - tes - moi ____
Tell me why ____

____ pour - quoi   la   vie est   bel - le,
____ the   sky   is filled with mu - sic,

C7

di - tes - moi _____ pour - quoi la vie est gai?
tell me why _____ we fly on clouds a - bove.

Di - tes - moi _____ pour - quoi, chère ma - d'moi
Can it be _____ that we can fly to

F   **Cdim/E♭**   **C/E**

sel - le, est - ce - que par - ce - que
mu - sic just be - cause, just be - cause

F6   **G7**   **1.** **C**   **G**   **2.** **C**

vous m'ai - mez? mez?
we're in love? love?

DO-RE-MI
from THE SOUND OF MUSIC

Lyrics by OSCAR HAMMERSTEIN II
Music by RICHARD RODGERS

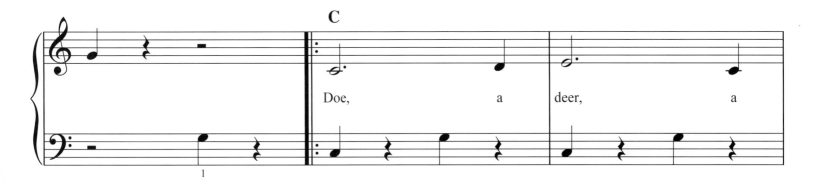

Me, a name I call my - self,

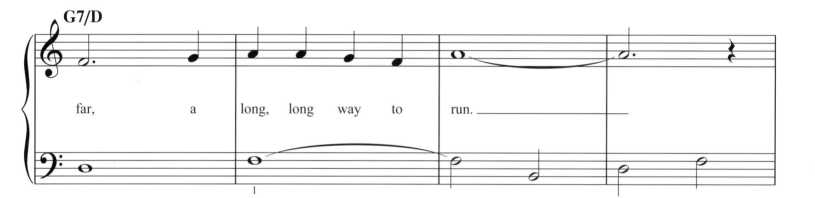

far, a long, long way to run. _____

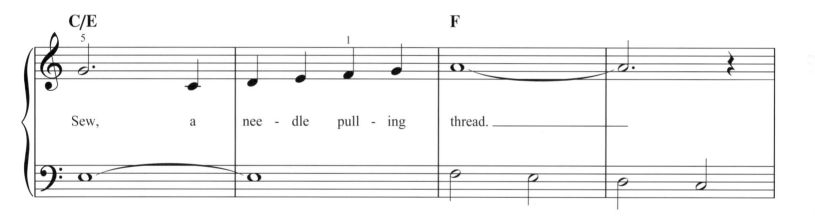

Sew, a nee - dle pull - ing thread. _____

La, a note to fol - low sew. _____

Tea, a drink with jam and

bread that will bring us back to

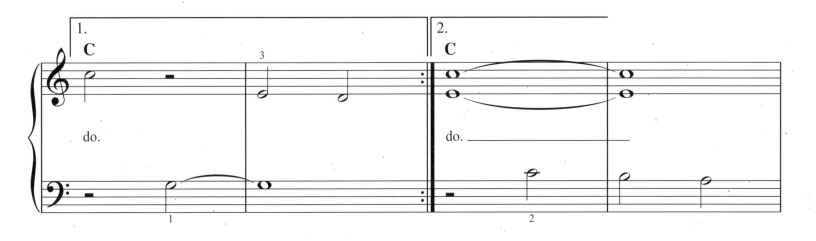

1. C
do.

2. C
do. _____

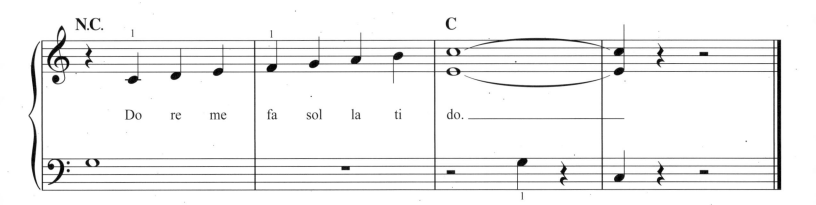

N.C.

Do re me fa sol la ti do. _____

GOD BLESS AMERICA®

Words and Music by
IRVING BERLIN

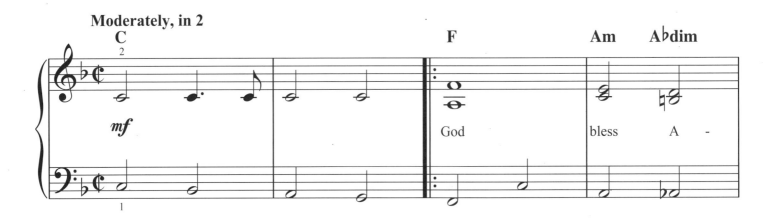

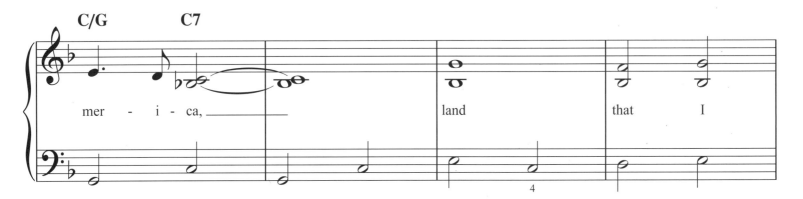

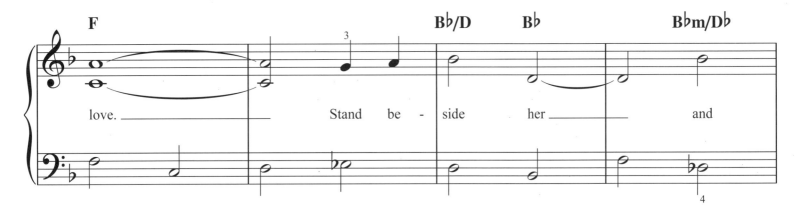

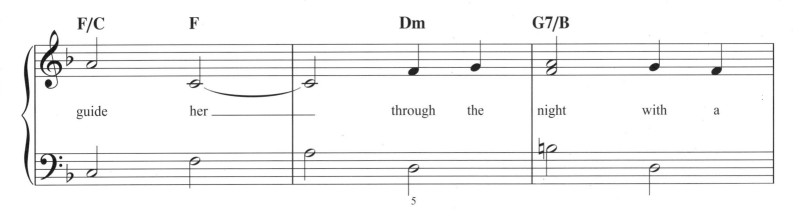

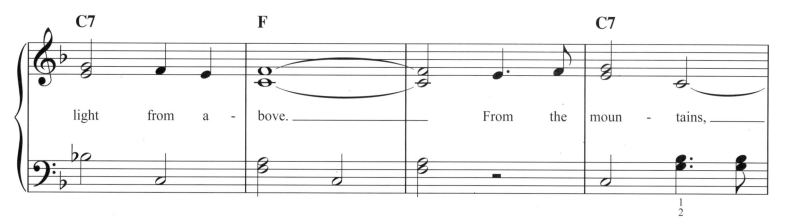

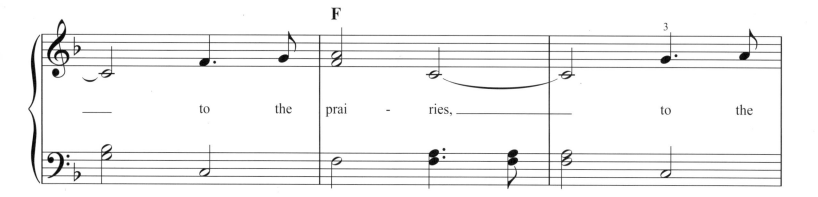

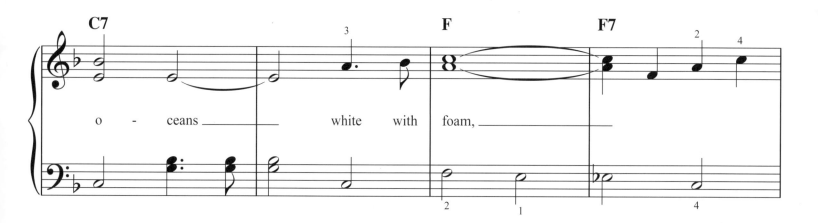

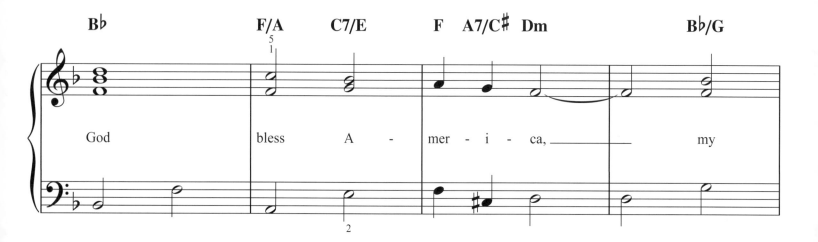

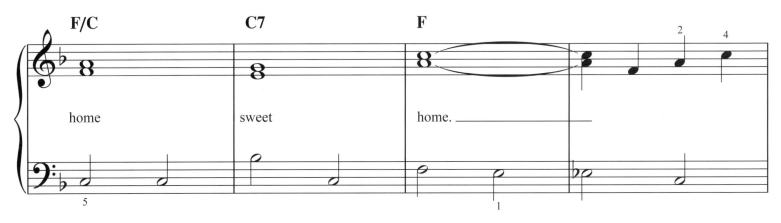

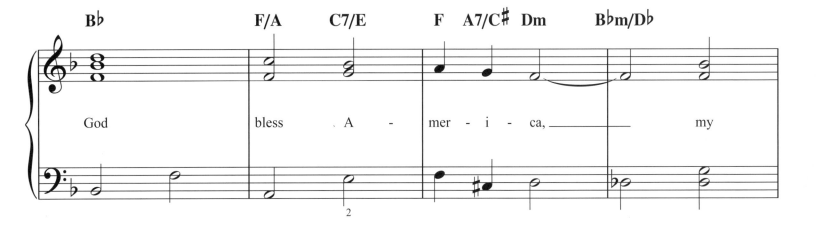

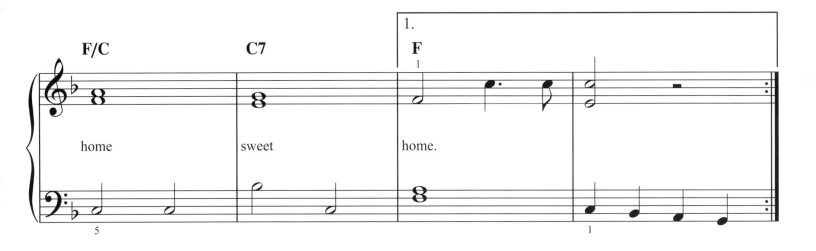

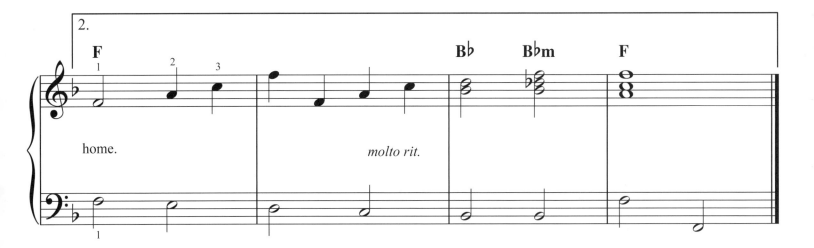

HAKUNA MATATA

from THE LION KING

Music by ELTON JOHN
Lyrics by TIM RICE

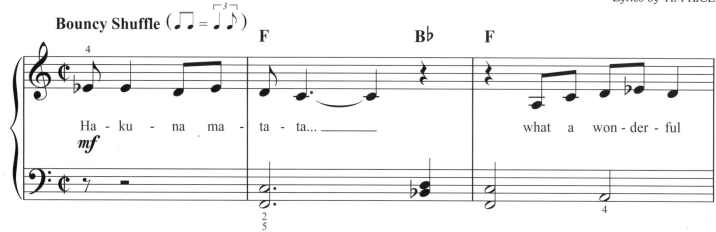

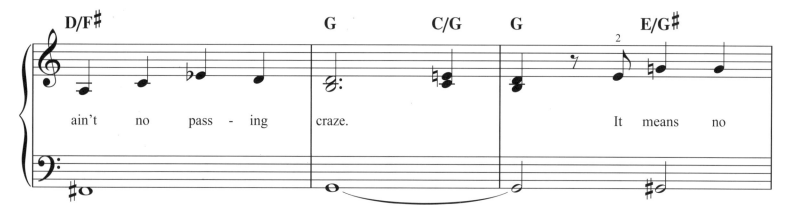

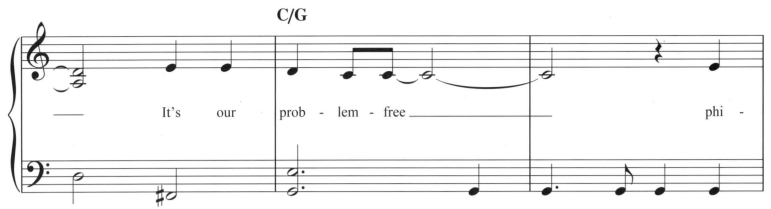

It's our prob - lem - free _____ phi -

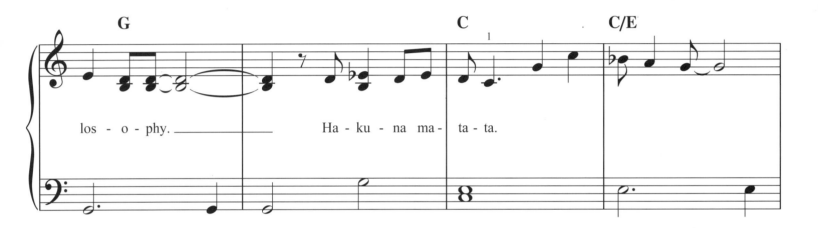

los - o - phy. _____ Ha - ku - na ma - ta - ta.

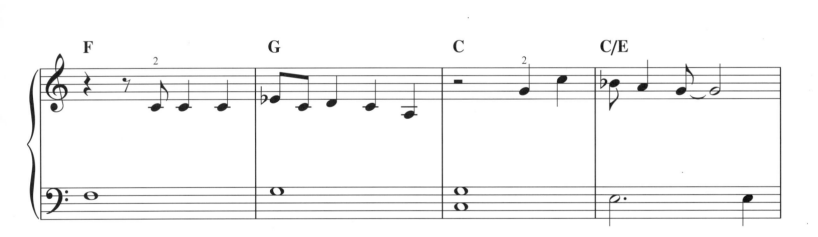

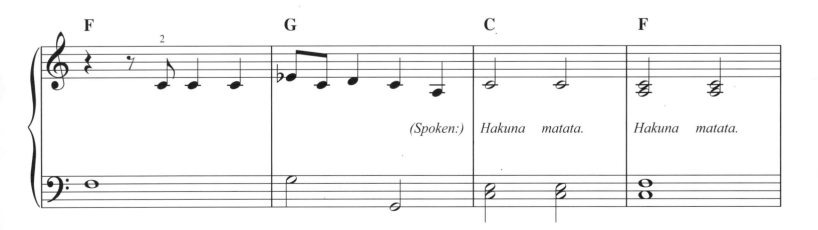

(Spoken:) Hakuna matata.   *Hakuna matata.*

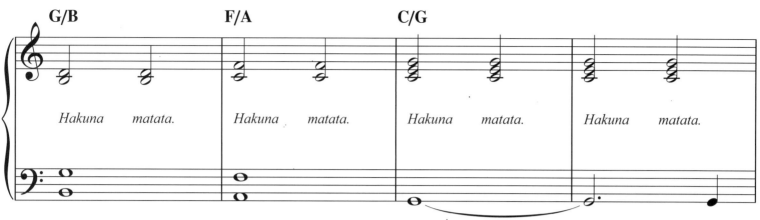

G/B   F/A   C/G

Hakuna matata.   *Hakuna matata.*   *Hakuna matata.*   *Hakuna matata.*

G   E/G♯   Am   C/E   F

Hakuna matata.   *(Sung:)*   *Hakuna...* It means no   wor - ries _____   for the rest ___ of your

D/F♯   C/G

days. _____   It's our   prob - lem - free _____   phi -

G7   E/G♯   Am

los - o - phy. ___   Ha - ku - na ma - ta - ta. _____

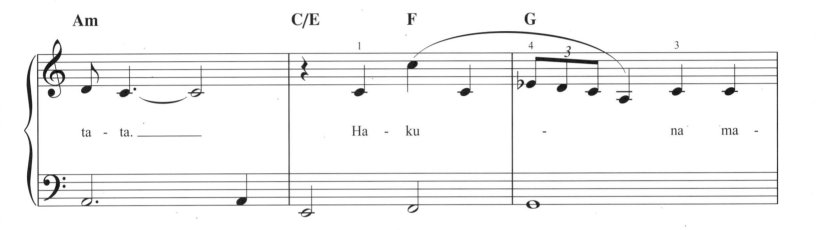

HAPPY BIRTHDAY TO YOU

Words and Music by MILDRED J. HILL
and PATTY S. HILL

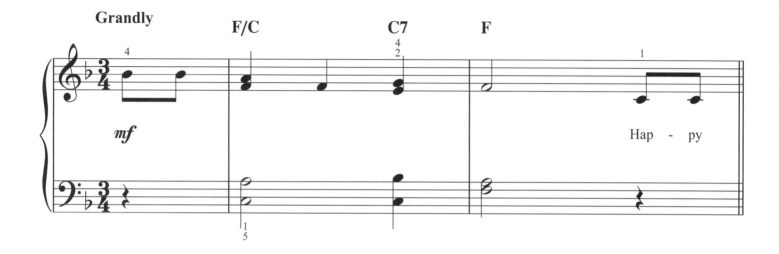

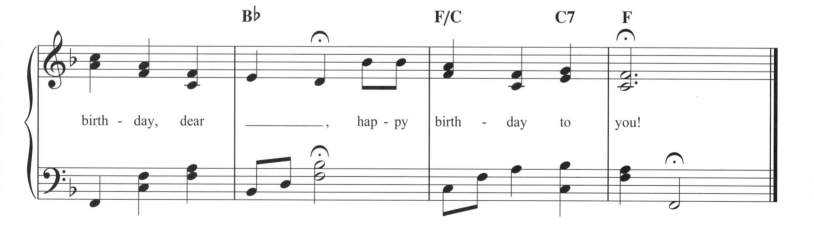

HERE WE GO LOOBY LOO

Traditional Folk Song

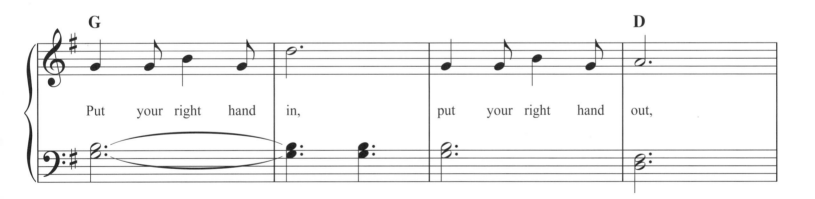

HAPPY TRAILS
from the Television Series THE ROY ROGERS SHOW

Words and Music by
DALE EVANS

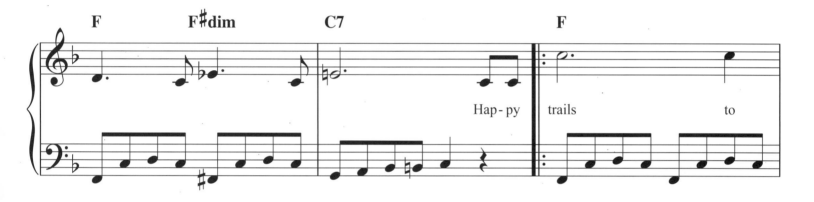

then. Who cares a - bout the clouds when we're to -

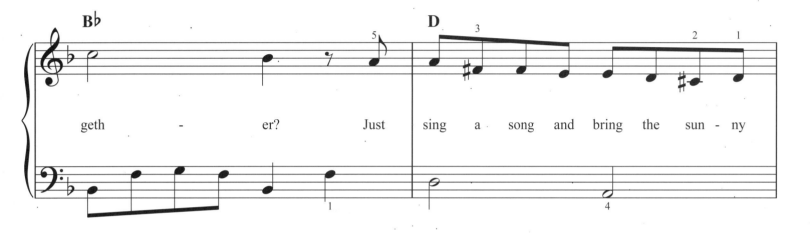

geth - er? Just sing a song and bring the sun - ny

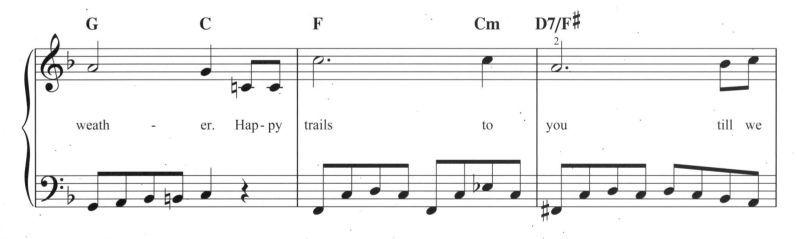

weath - er. Hap - py trails to you till we

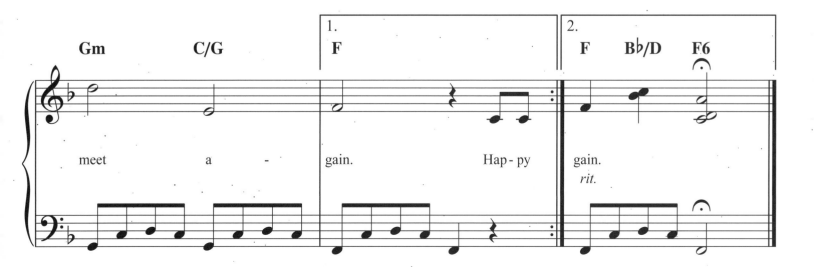

meet a - gain. Hap - py gain.

HEART AND SOUL
from the Paramount Short Subject A SONG IS BORN

Words by FRANK LOESSER
Music by HOAGY CARMICHAEL

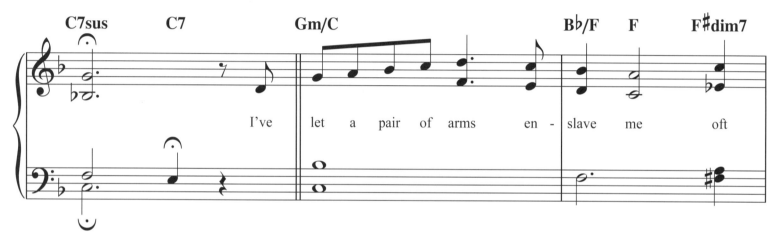

I've let a pair of arms en - slave me oft

times be - fore, but more than just a thrill you

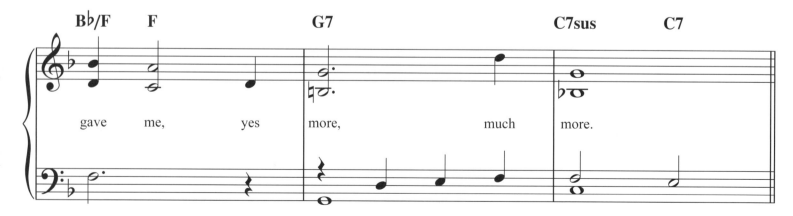

gave me, yes more, much more.

Moderately (♪♪ = ♪♪³)

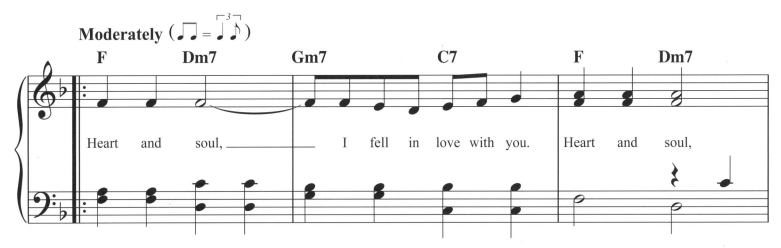

Heart and soul, _____ I fell in love with you. Heart and soul,

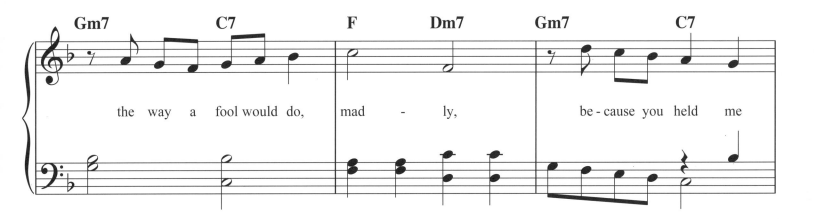

the way a fool would do, mad - ly, be - cause you held me

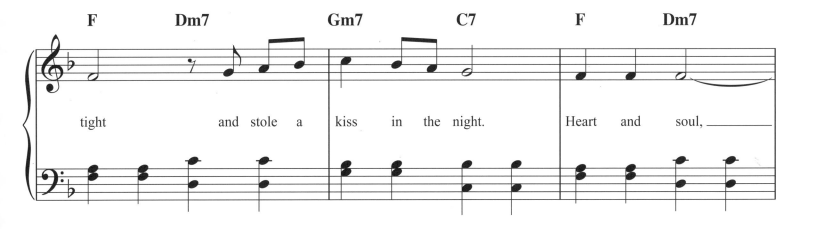

tight and stole a kiss in the night. Heart and soul, _____

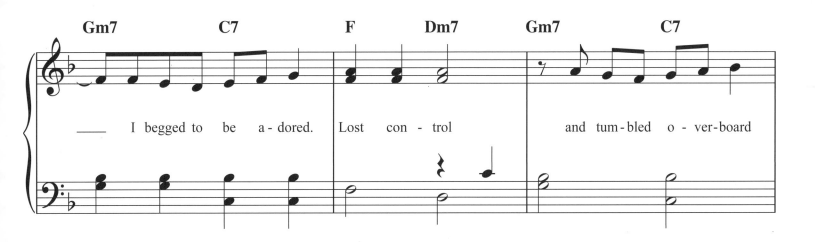

_____ I begged to be a - dored. Lost con - trol and tum - bled o - ver-board

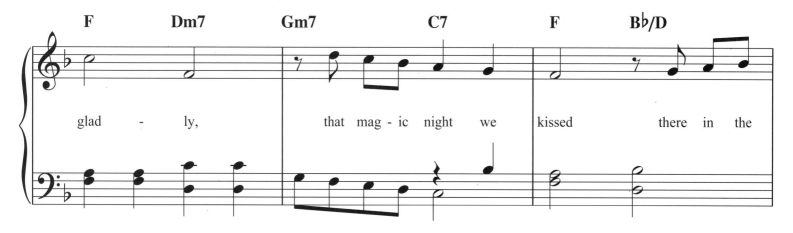

glad - ly,   that mag - ic night we   kissed   there in the

moon - mist.   Oh! but your lips   were thrill - ing,

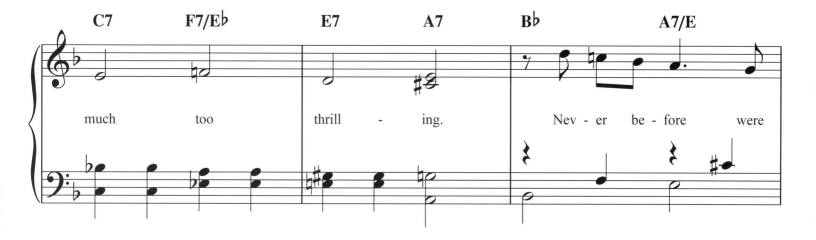

much   too   thrill - ing.   Nev - er be - fore were

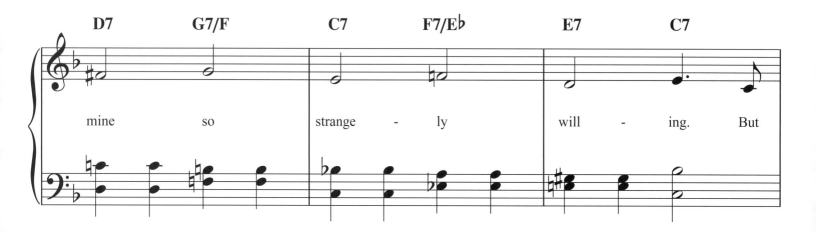

mine   so   strange - ly   will - ing. But

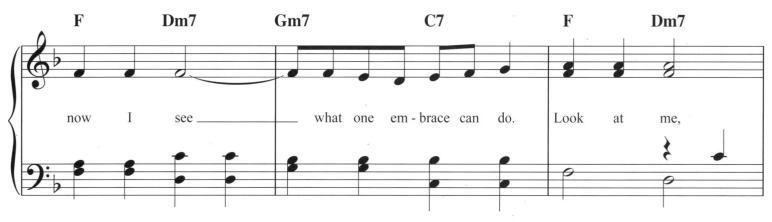

now I see _____ what one em-brace can do. Look at me,

it's got me lov-ing you mad - ly, that lit-tle kiss you

1.

stole held all my heart and soul.

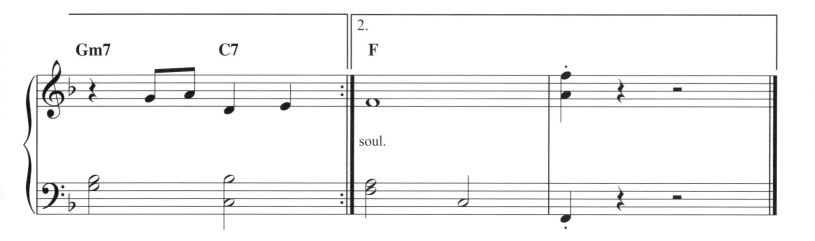

2.

soul.

THE HOKEY POKEY

Words and Music by CHARLES P. MACAK,
TAFFT BAKER and LARRY LaPRISE

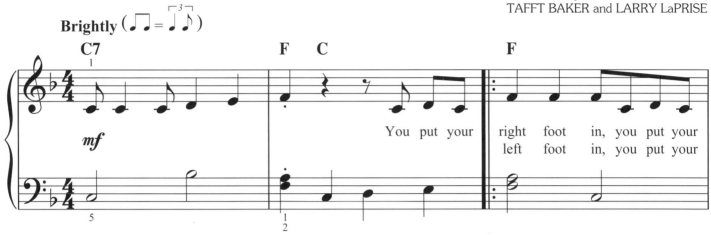

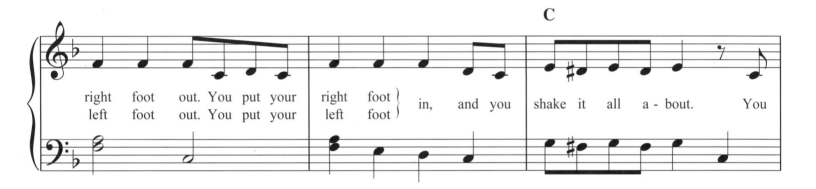

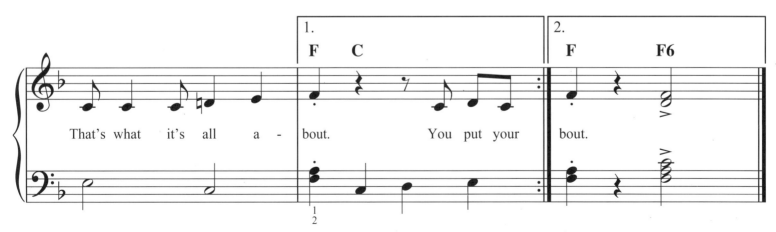

IF I ONLY HAD A BRAIN
from THE WIZARD OF OZ

Lyric by E.Y. "YIP" HARBURG
Music by HAROLD ARLEN

I could wile a-way the hours __ con-
man's an emp-ty ket-tle he
sad, be-lieve me, mis-sy, when you're

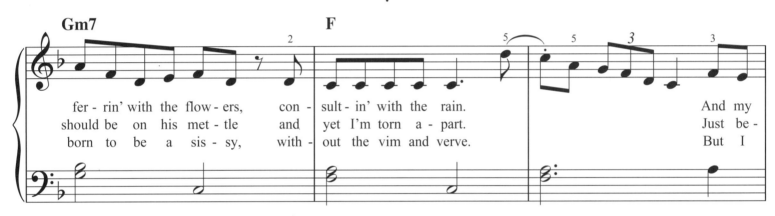

fer-rin' with the flow-ers, con - sult-in' with the rain. And my
should be on his met-tle and yet I'm torn a-part. Just be-
born to be a sis-sy, with - out the vim and verve. But I

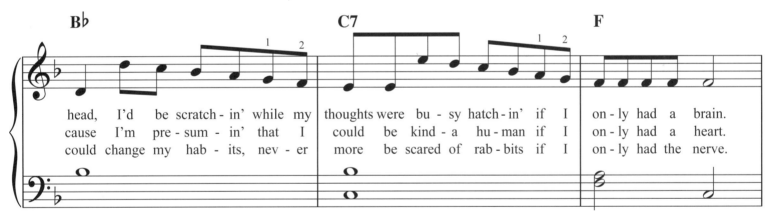

head, I'd be scratch-in' while my thoughts were bu-sy hatch-in' if I on-ly had a brain.
cause I'm pre-sum-in' that I could be kind-a hu-man if I on-ly had a heart.
could change my hab-its, nev-er more be scared of rab-bits if I on-ly had the nerve.

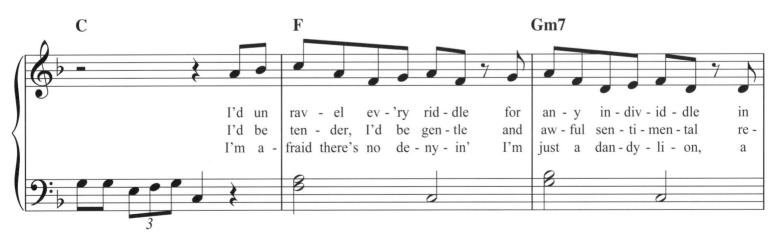

I'd un - rav-el ev-'ry rid-dle for an-y in-div-id-dle in
I'd be ten-der, I'd be gen-tle and aw-ful sen-ti-men-tal re-
I'm a - fraid there's no de-ny-in' I'm just a dan-dy-li-on, a

trou - ble or in pain. / gard - ing love and art. / fate I don't de - serve. With the I'd be But I thoughts I'd be think - in' I could / friends with the spar - rows and the / could show my prow - ess, be a

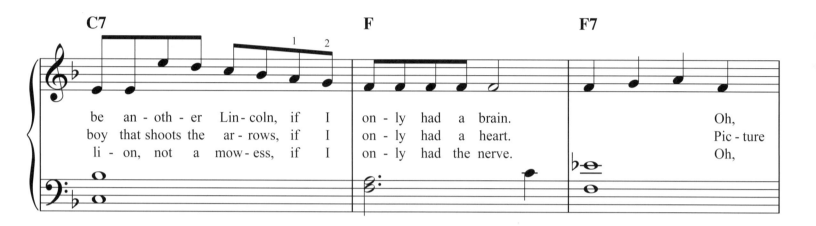

be an - oth - er Lin - coln, if I / boy that shoots the ar - rows, if I / li - on, not a mow - ess, if I on - ly had a brain. / on - ly had a heart. / on - ly had the nerve. Oh, / Pic - ture / Oh,

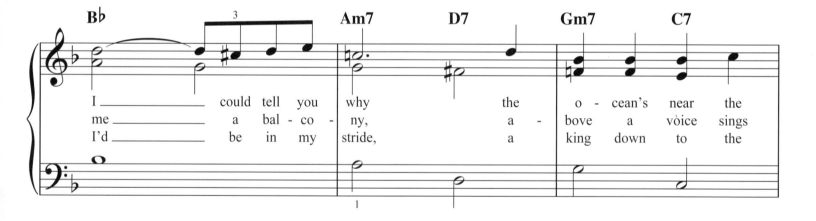

I _____ could tell you / me _____ a bal - co - / I'd _____ be in my why / ny, / stride, the / a - / a o - cean's near the / bove a voice sings / king down to the

shore. I could / low, "Where - fore / core. Oh, I'd think of things I nev - er thunk be - / art thou, Ro - me - / roar the way I nev - er roared be - fore, / o?" / fore, and then I'd / I hear a / and then I'd

sit and think some more. I would not be just a nuff-in' my
beat. How sweet! Just to reg - is - ter e - mo - tion,
rrrwoof, and roar some more. I would show the di - no - sau - rus who's

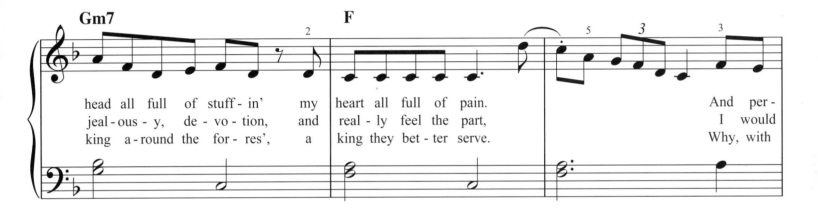

head all full of stuff - in' my heart all full of pain. And per -
jeal - ous - y, de - vo - tion, and real - ly feel the part, I would
king a - round the for - res', a king they bet - ter serve. Why, with

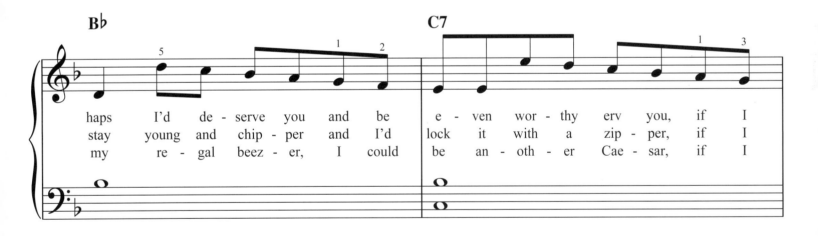

haps I'd de - serve you and be e - ven wor - thy erv you, if I
stay young and chip - per and I'd lock it with a zip - per, if I
my re - gal beez - er, I could be an - oth - er Cae - sar, if I

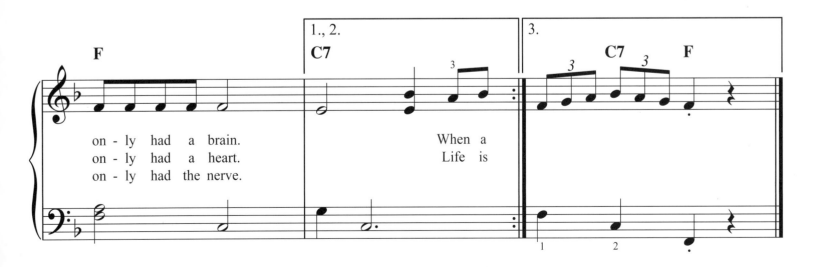

on - ly had a brain.
on - ly had a heart.
on - ly had the nerve.

When a
Life is

IF YOU'RE HAPPY AND YOU KNOW IT

Words and Music by
L. SMITH

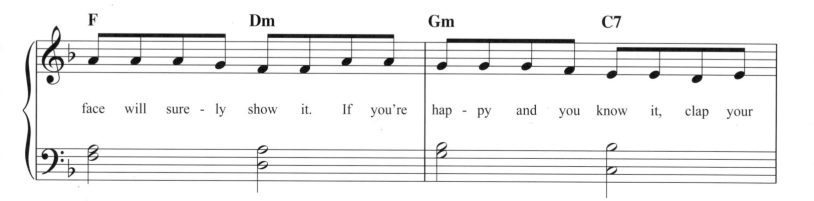

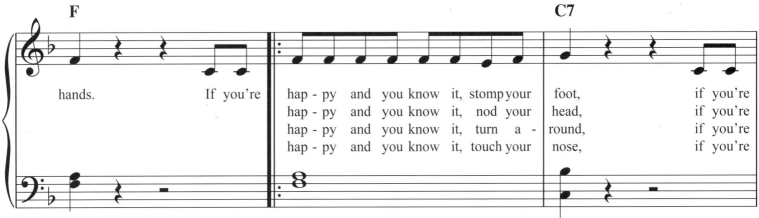

hands. If you're | hap-py and you know it, stomp your **foot,** if you're
hap-py and you know it, nod your **head,** if you're
hap-py and you know it, turn a-**round,** if you're
hap-py and you know it, touch your **nose,** if you're

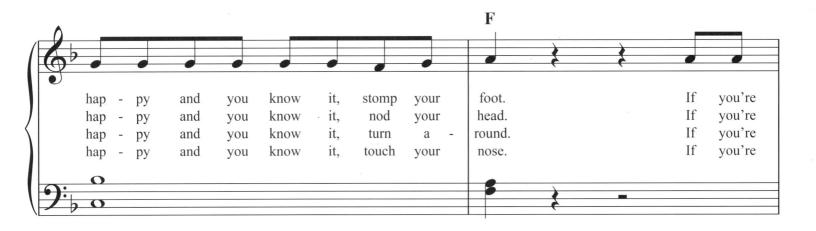

hap-py and you know it, stomp your **foot.** If you're
hap-py and you know it, nod your **head.** If you're
hap-py and you know it, turn a-**round.** If you're
hap-py and you know it, touch your **nose.** If you're

hap-py and you know it, then your face will sure-ly show it. If you're
hap-py and you know it, then your face will sure-ly show it. If you're
hap-py and you know it, then your face will sure-ly show it. If you're
hap-py and you know it, then your face will sure-ly show it. If you're

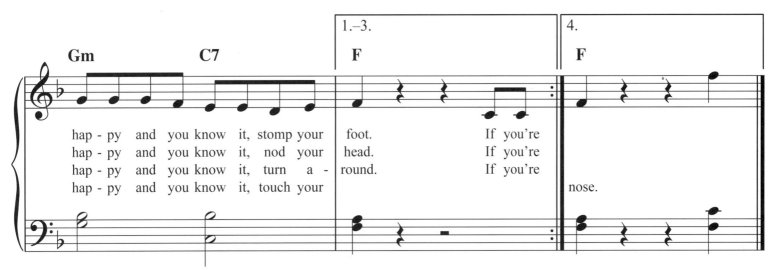

hap-py and you know it, stomp your | **foot.** If you're
hap-py and you know it, nod your | **head.** If you're
hap-py and you know it, turn a- | **round.** If you're
hap-py and you know it, touch your | **nose.**

KUM BA YAH

Traditional Spiritual

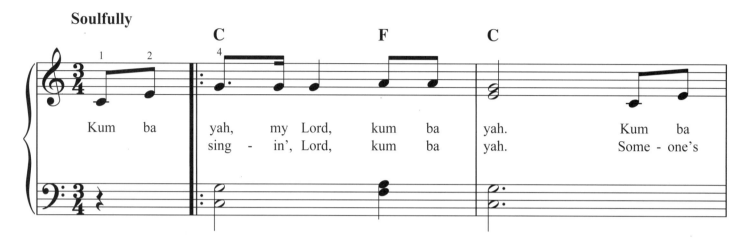

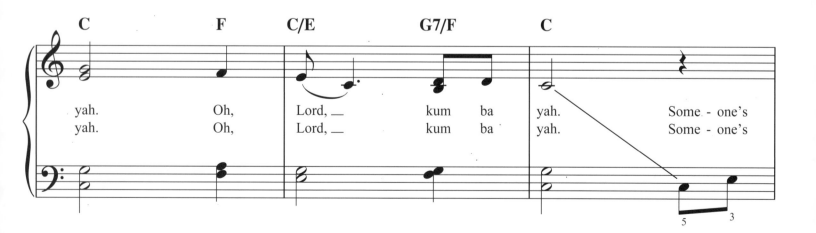

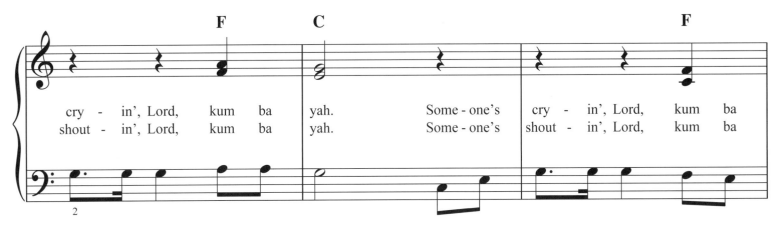

cry - in', Lord, kum ba yah. Some - one's cry - in', Lord, kum ba
shout - in', Lord, kum ba yah. Some - one's shout - in', Lord, kum ba

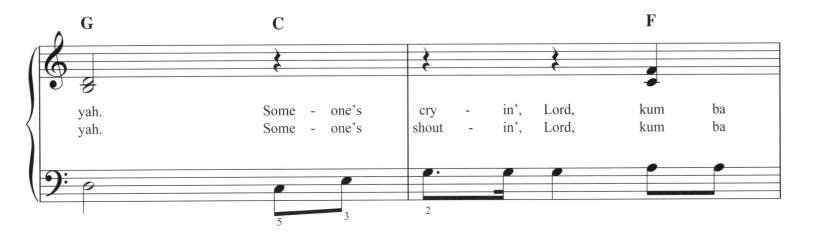

yah. Some - one's cry - in', Lord, kum ba
yah. Some - one's shout - in', Lord, kum ba

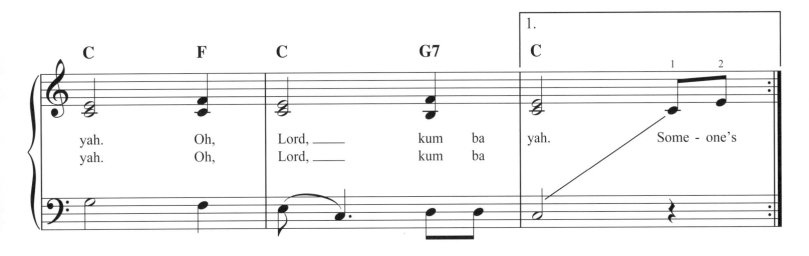

yah. Oh, Lord, _____ kum ba yah. Some - one's
yah. Oh, Lord, _____ kum ba

1.

2.

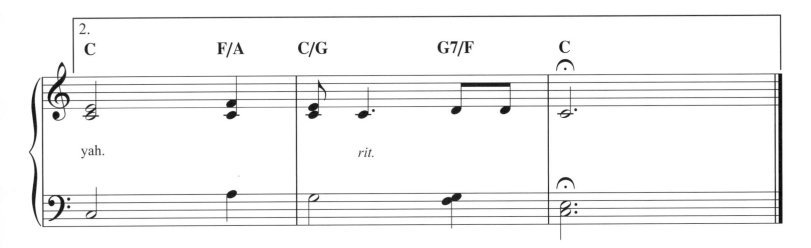

yah.

rit.

LET IT GO
from FROZEN

Music and Lyrics by KRISTEN ANDERSON-LOPEZ
and ROBERT LOPEZ

Half-time feel, mysterious

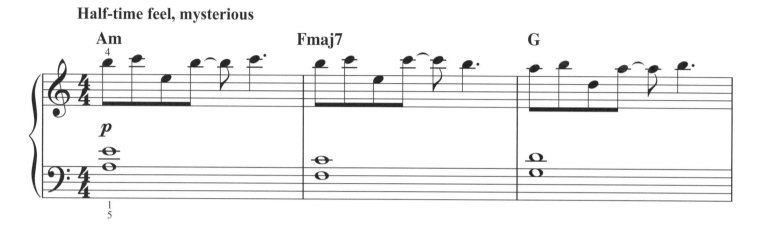

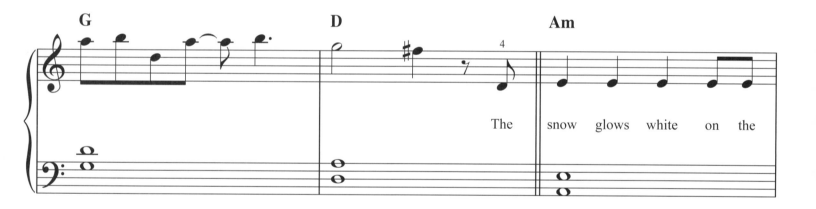

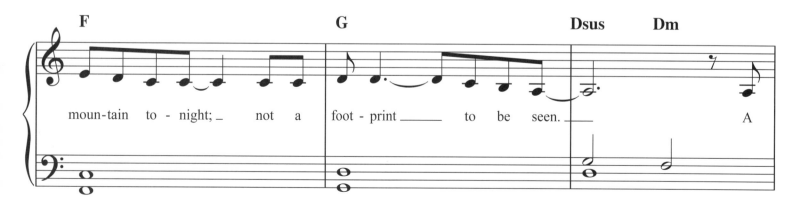

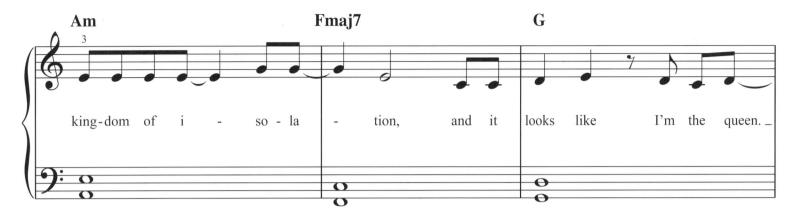

king-dom of i - so - la - tion, and it looks like I'm the queen.

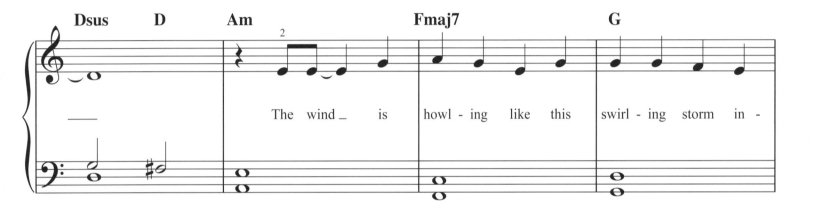

_ The wind _ is howl - ing like this swirl - ing storm in -

side. _____ Could - n't keep it in, _____ heav - en knows I _____

_ tried. Don't let _ them in, don't let them

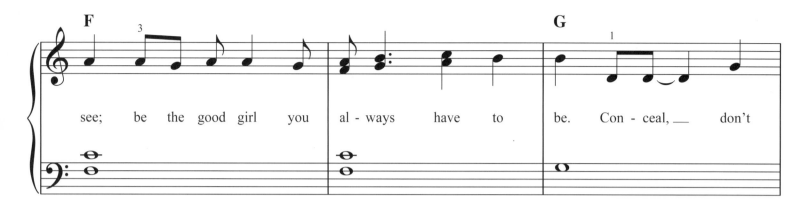

see; be the good girl you al-ways have to be. Con-ceal,___ don't

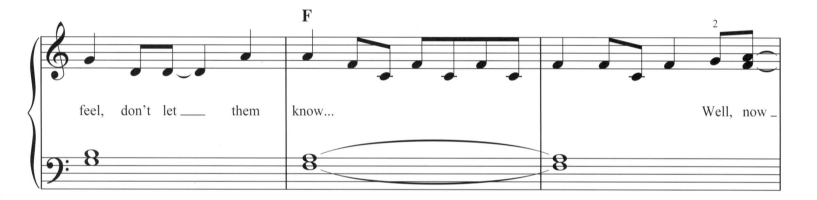

feel, don't let ___ them know... Well, now ___

they know. ___ Let it go, ___ let it go; ___
let it go; ___

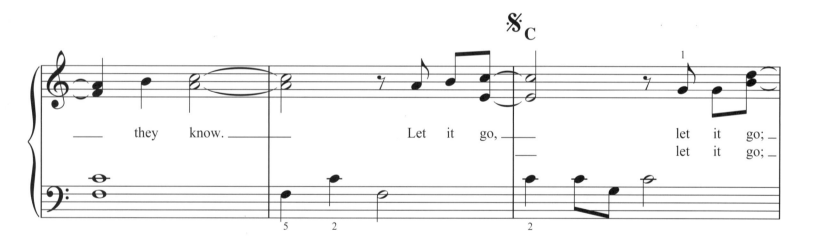

can't ___ hold it back an-y-more. ___ Let it go, ___
I am one with the wind and sky. ___ Let it go,

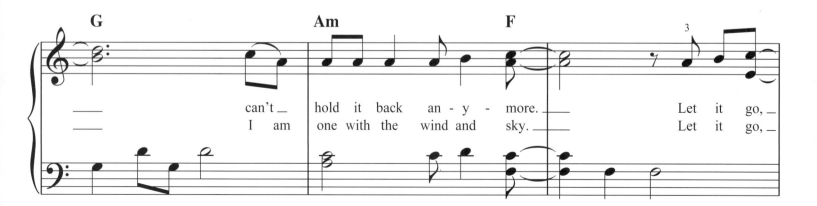

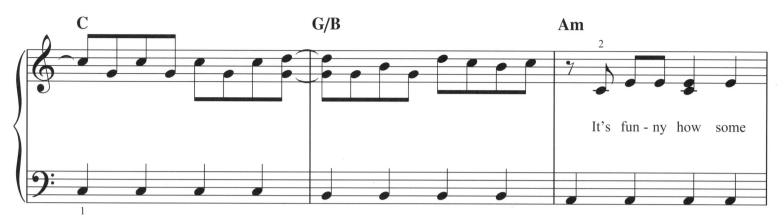

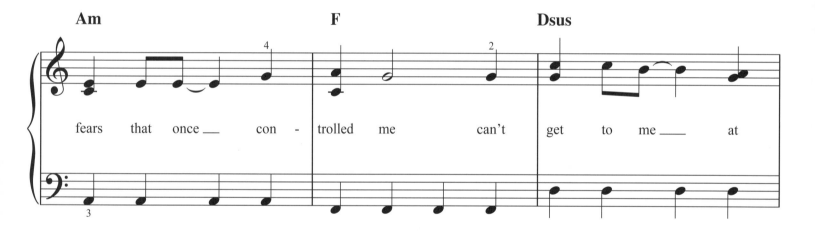

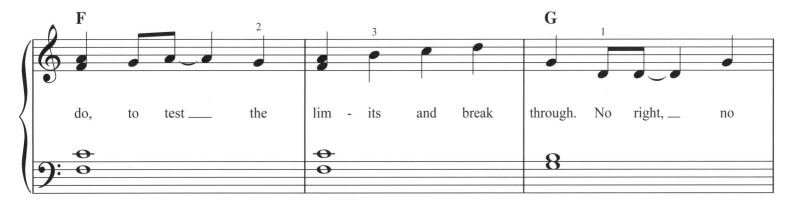

do, to test ____ the lim - its and break through. No right, ___ no

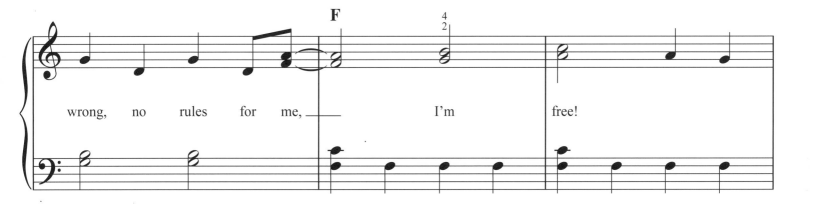

wrong, no rules for me, ____ I'm free!

D.S. al Coda

Let it go, ___

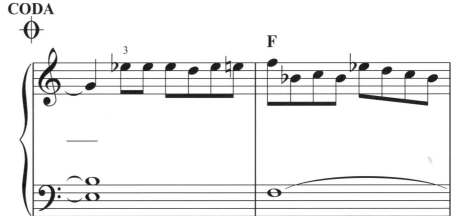

CODA

My pow - er   flur - ries through the   air in - to the

ground.   My soul __ is   spi - ral - ing in

G

fro - zen frac - tals   all a - round. __   And one __ thought

cry - stal - liz - es   like an i - cy   blast:

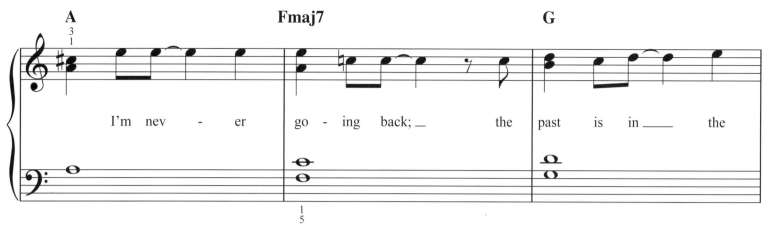

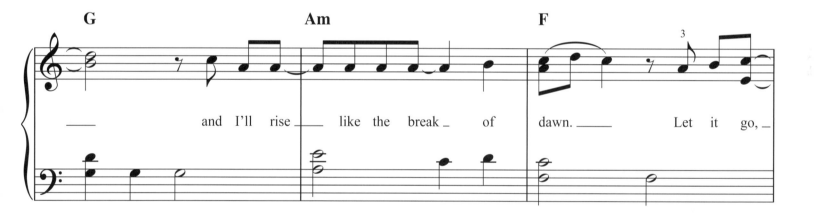

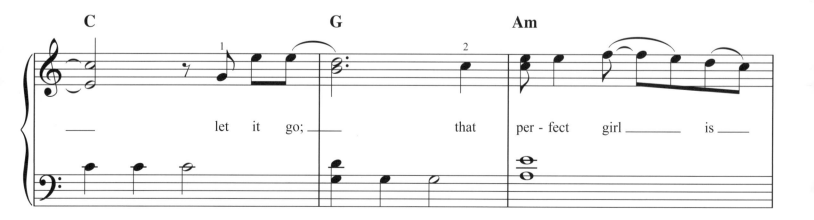

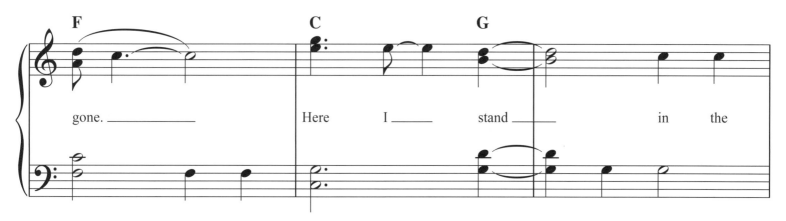

gone.＿＿＿＿ Here I ＿＿ stand ＿＿＿ in the

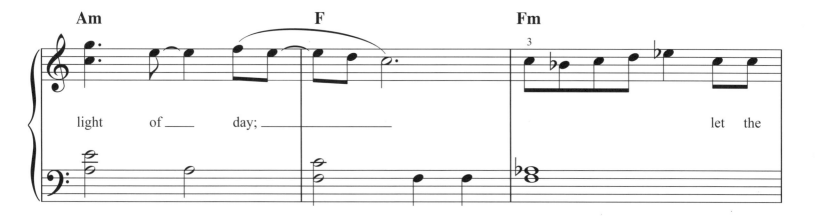

light of ＿＿ day; ＿＿＿＿＿＿＿ let the

storm rage ＿ on. ＿＿＿ The

cold nev - er both - ered me an - y - way. ＿＿＿

LITTLE BROWN JUG

Words and Music by
JOSEPH E. WINNER

My wife and I, we live a-lone in a

lit-tle log hut we call our own. Here you are so near my nose, I tip her up and

down she goes. Ha ha ha, you and me, lit-tle brown jug how I love thee.

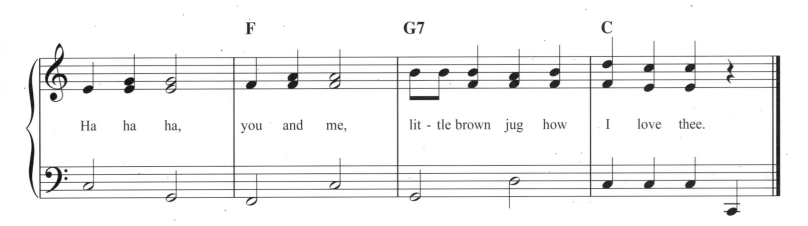

Ha ha ha, you and me, lit-tle brown jug how I love thee.

LINUS AND LUCY

By VINCE GUARALDI

Brightly

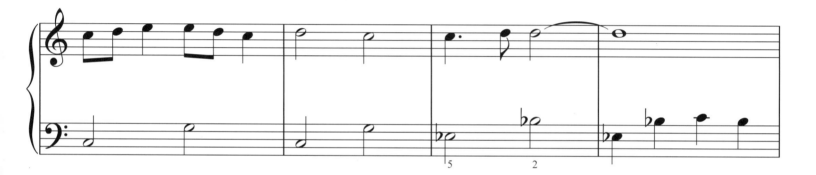

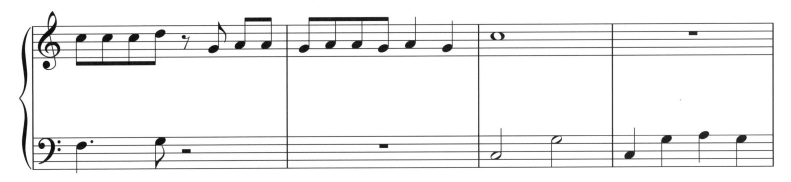

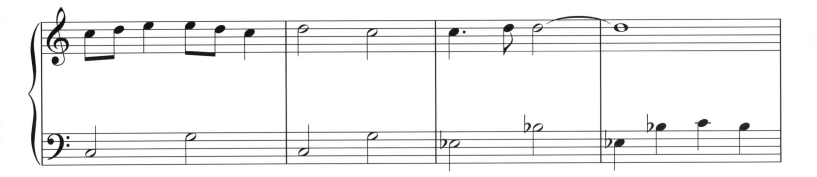

LITTLE PEOPLE
from LES MISÉRABLES

Music by CLAUDE-MICHEL SCHÖNBERG
Lyrics by ALAIN BOUBLIL,
JEAN-MARC NATEL and HERBERT KRETZMER

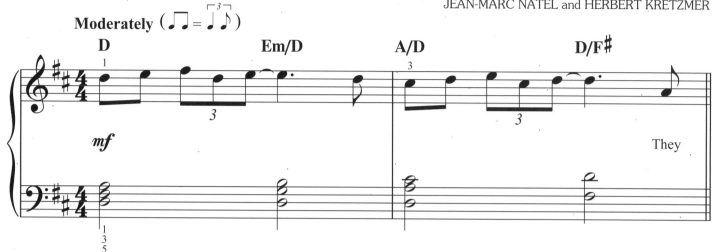

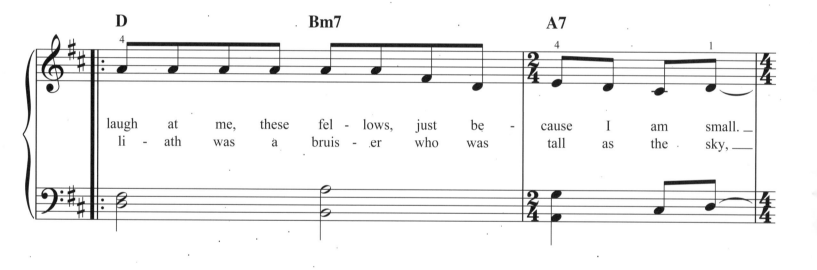

I tell 'em there's a lot to learn down
I nev-er read the Bi-ble, but I

here on the ground. ___
know that it's true. ___
The
It

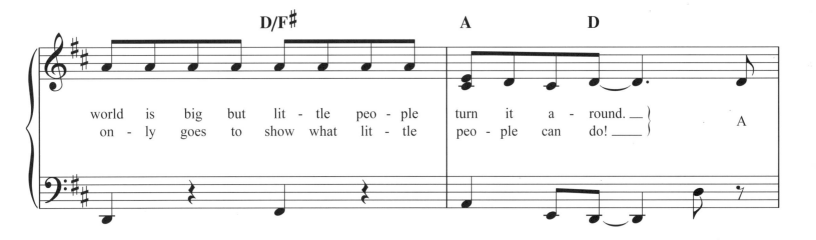

world is big but lit-tle peo-ple
on-ly goes to show what lit-tle
turn it a-round. ___
peo-ple can do! ___
A

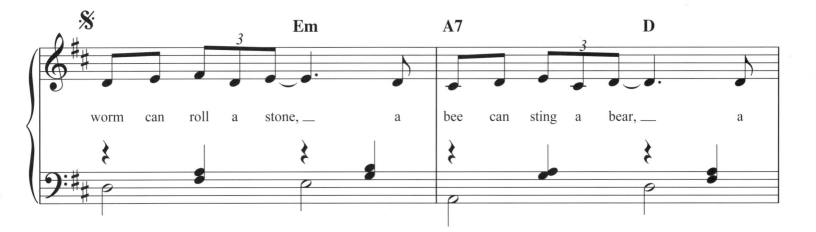

worm can roll a stone, ___ a
bee can sting a bear, ___ a

fly can fly a-round Ver - sailles 'cos flies don't care! __ A spar-row in a hat can

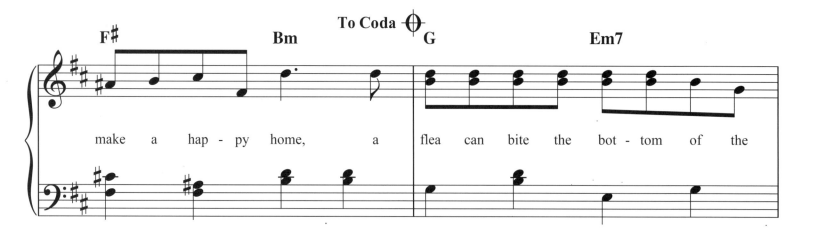

make a hap - py home, a flea can bite the bot - tom of the

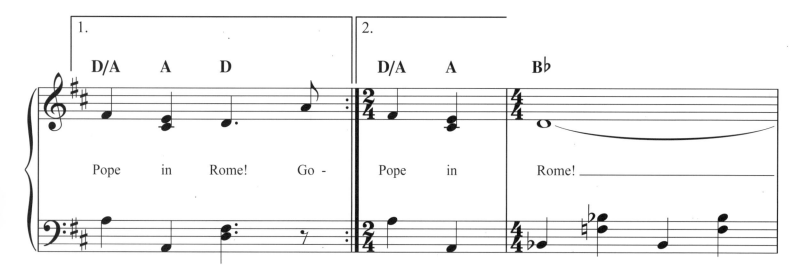

Pope in Rome! Go - Pope in Rome! __

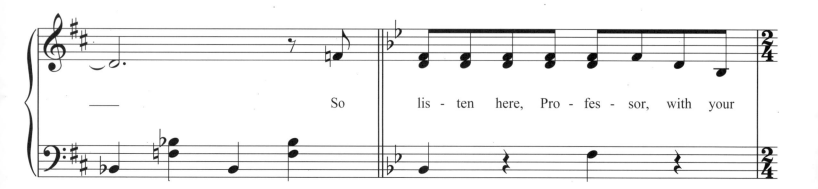

__ So lis - ten here, Pro - fes - sor, with your

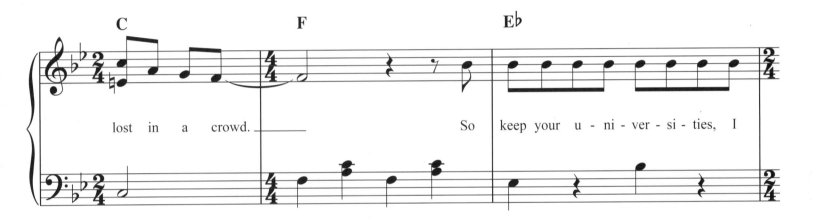

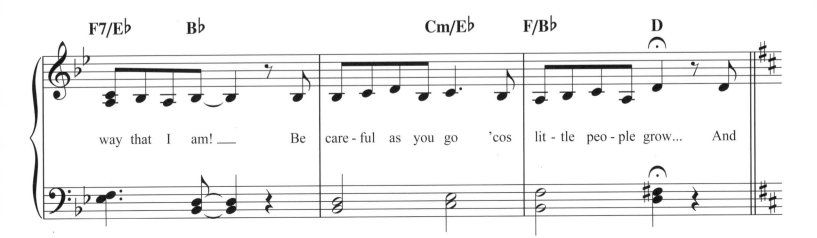

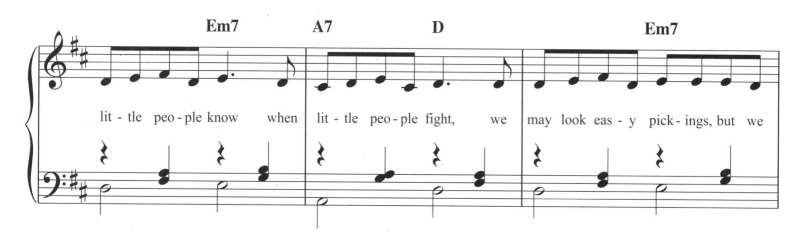

little peo-ple know when lit-tle peo-ple fight, we may look eas-y pick-ings, but we

got some bite! So nev-er kick a dog be-cause it's just a pup. You

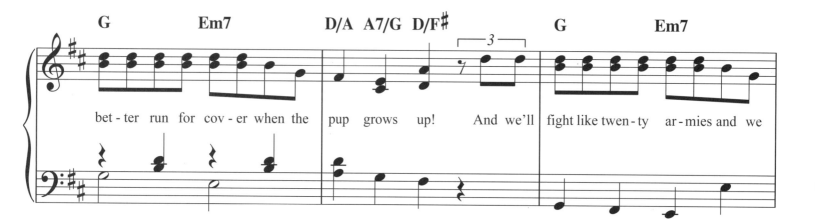

bet-ter run for cov-er when the pup grows up! And we'll fight like twen-ty ar-mies and we

won't give up! A

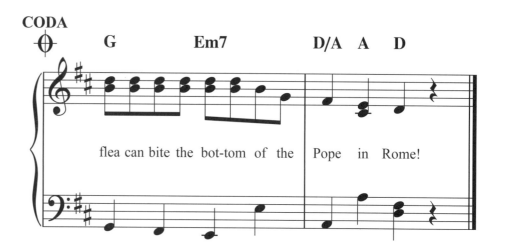

flea can bite the bot-tom of the Pope in Rome!

ON TOP OF SPAGHETTI

Words and Music by
TOM GLAZER

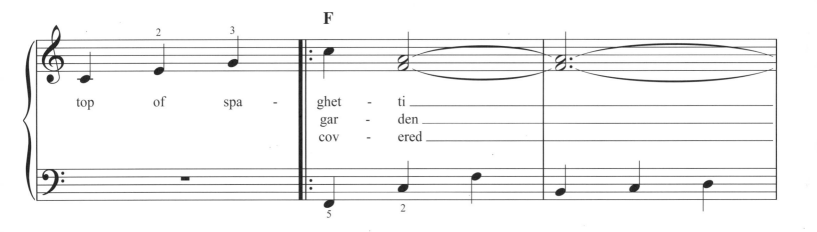

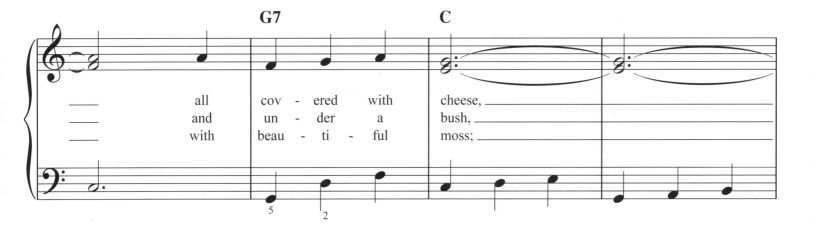

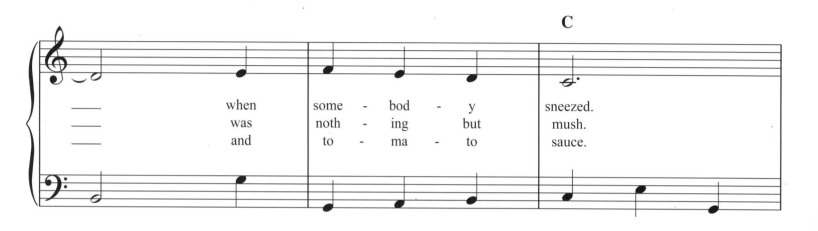

G7

I lost my poor meat - ball ___
and then my poor meat - ball ___
it grew love - ly meat - balls ___

5

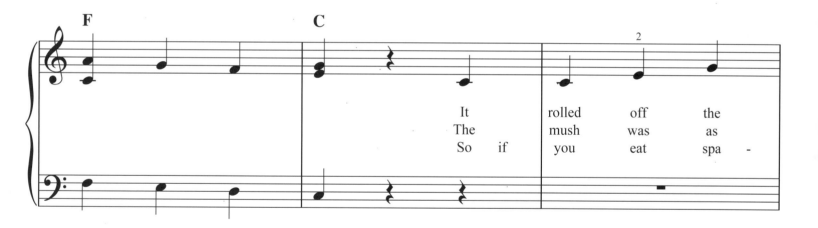

C

when some - bod - y sneezed.
was noth - ing but mush.
and to - ma - to sauce.

F   **C**

2

It rolled off the
The mush was as
So if you eat spa -

F   **G7**

ta - ble ___ and on - to the
tast - y ___ as tast - y could
ghet - ti ___ all cov - ered with

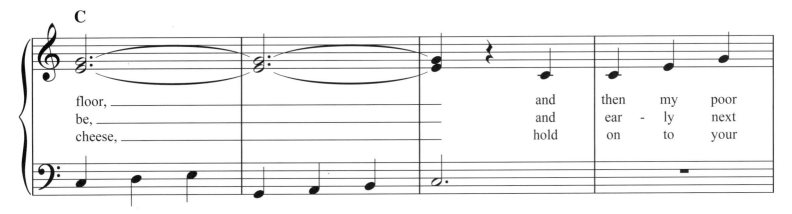

floor,
be,
cheese,

and
and
hold

then
ear -
on

my
ly
to

poor
next
your

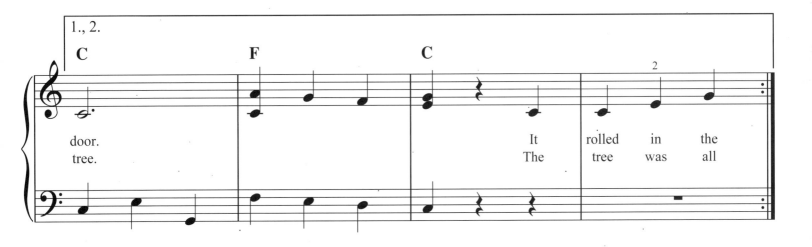

meat - ball
sum - mer,
meat - balls

rolled
it grew
and

out
in -
don't

of
to
ev -

the
a
er

1., 2.

door.
tree.

It
The

rolled
tree

in
was

the
all

3.

sneeze.

A - choo!

MY FAVORITE THINGS
from THE SOUND OF MUSIC

Lyrics by OSCAR HAMMERSTEIN II
Music by RICHARD RODGERS

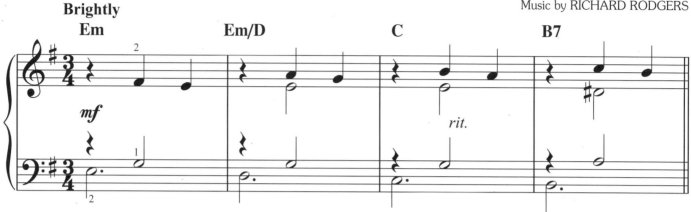

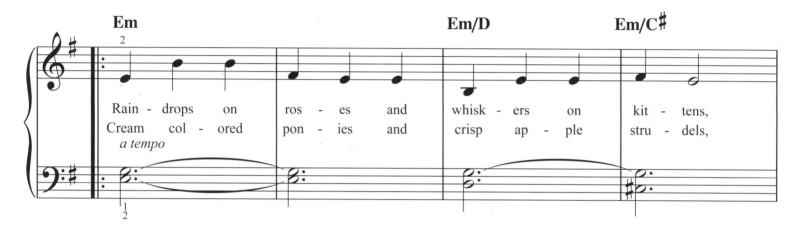

Rain - drops on ros - es and whisk - ers on kit - tens,
Cream col - ored pon - ies and crisp ap - ple stru - dels,

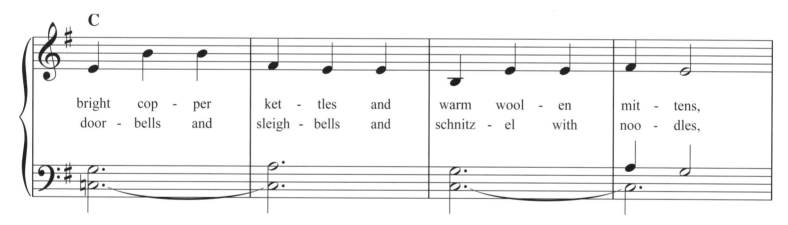

bright cop - per ket - tles and warm wool - en mit - tens,
door - bells and sleigh - bells and schnitz - el with noo - dles,

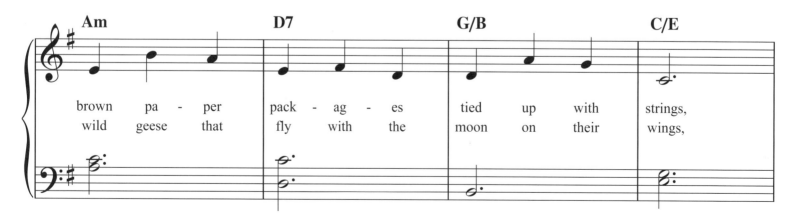

brown pa - per pack - ag - es tied up with strings,
wild geese that fly with the moon on their wings,

these are a few of my fa - vor - ite things.
these are a few of my fa - vor - ite things.

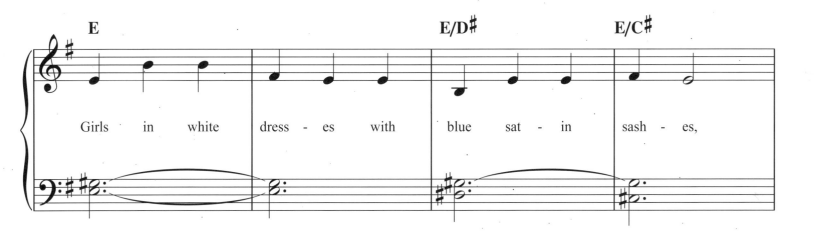

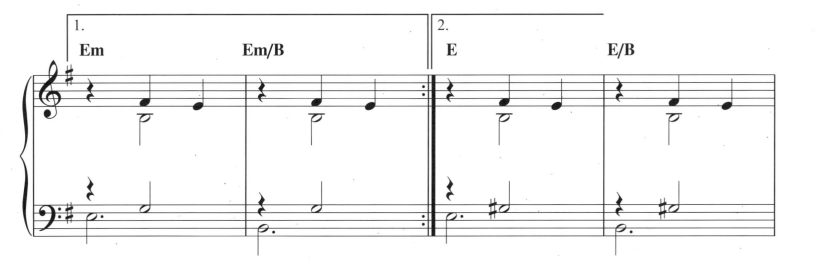

Girls in white dress - es with blue sat - in sash - es,

snow - flakes that stay on my nose and eye - lash - es,

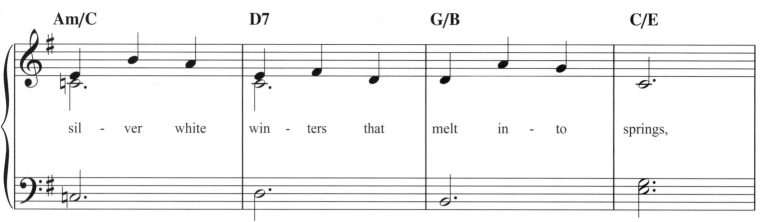

sil - ver white win - ters that melt in - to springs,

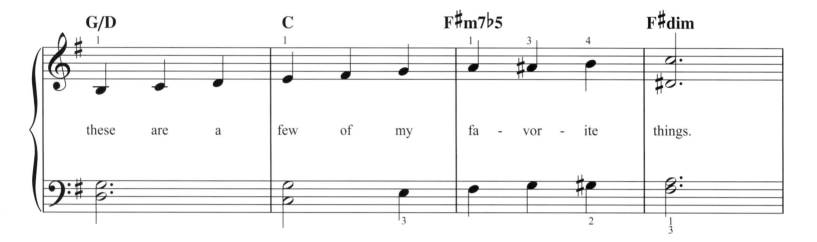

these are a few of my fa - vor - ite things.

When the dog bites, when the bee stings,

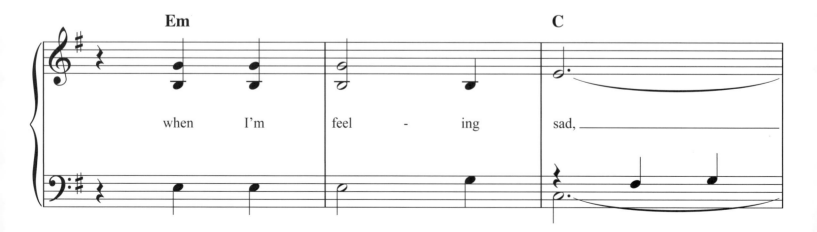

when I'm feel - ing sad, _____

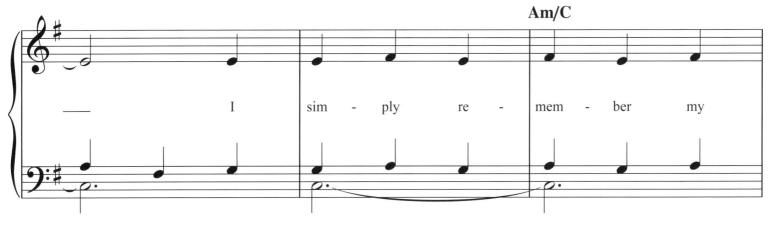

Am/C

I sim - ply re - mem - ber my

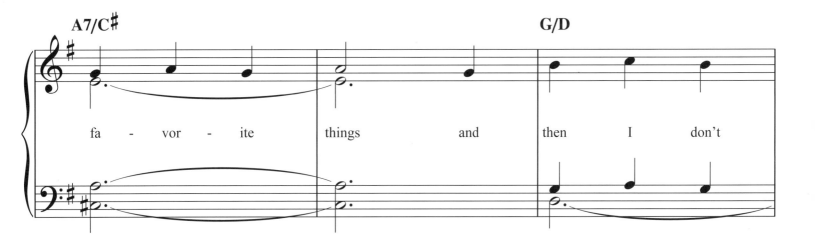

A7/C♯　　　　　　　　　　　　　　　　　　**G/D**

fa - vor - ite　　things　　and　　then　　I　　don't

D7　　　　**D7♭9**　　**D9**　　**G**

feel　　　　　　　　so　　bad.

B♭/D　　　　　　　　　**D7**　　　　　　**G**

OCTOPUS'S GARDEN

Words and Music by
RICHARD STARKEY

I'd like to be ___
We would be warm ___

un - der the sea ___
be - low the storm ___

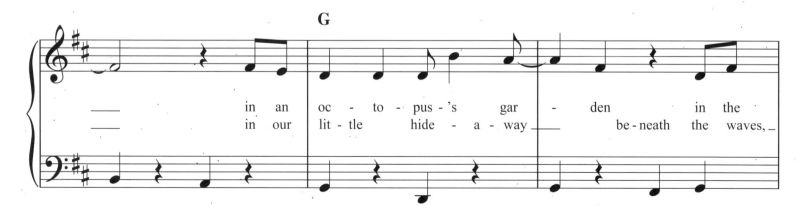

___ in an oc - to - pus - 's gar - den in the
___ in our lit - tle hide - a - way ___ be - neath the waves,

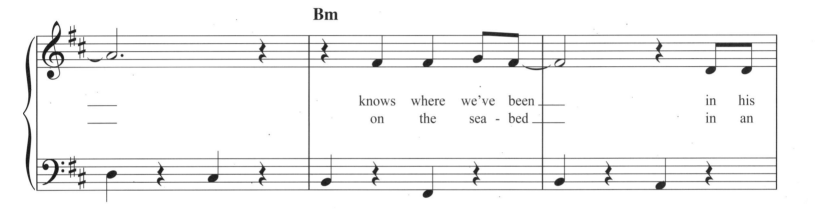

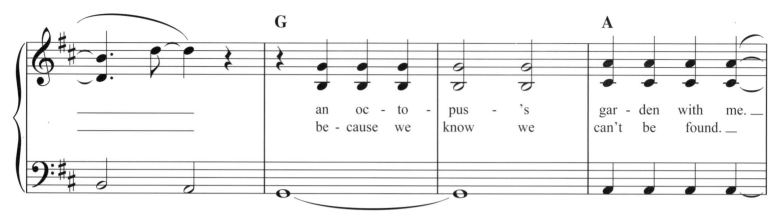

an oc - to - pus - 's   gar - den with me. ___
be - cause we know we can't be found. ___

I'd like to be ___   un - der the sea ___

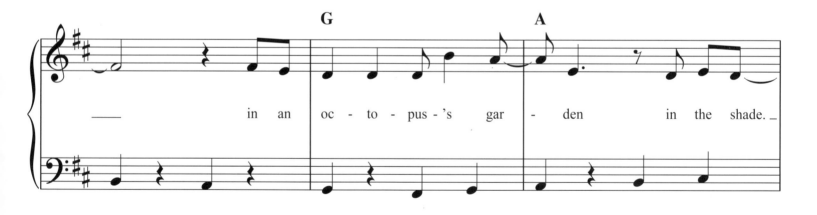

___ in an oc - to - pus - 's gar - den   in the shade. ___

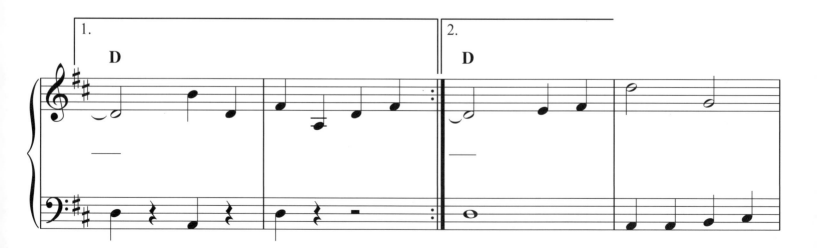

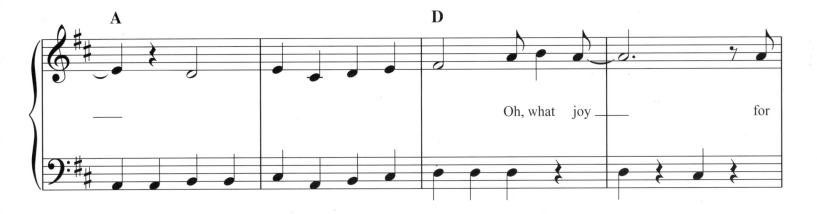

hap - py   and they're   safe.   We would

be   so   hap - py   you   and   me;

no   one   there   to   tell   us   what   to   do.

I'd   like   to   be

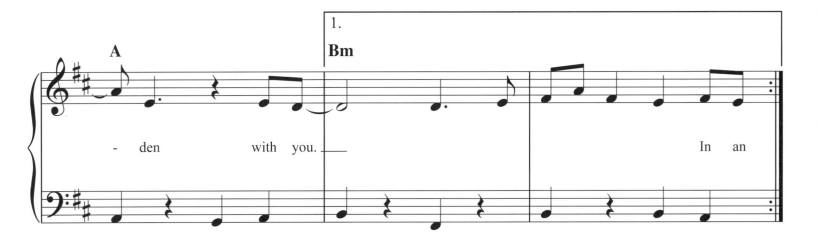

SING
from SESAME STREET

Words and Music by
JOE RAPOSO

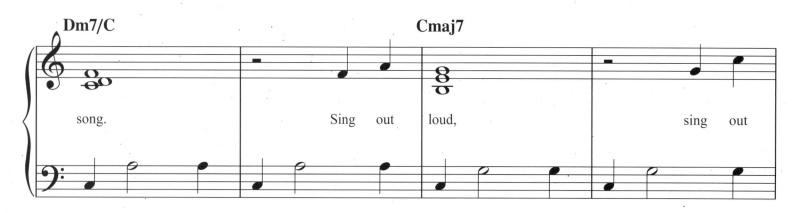

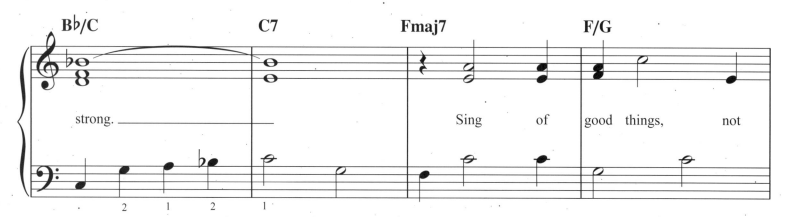

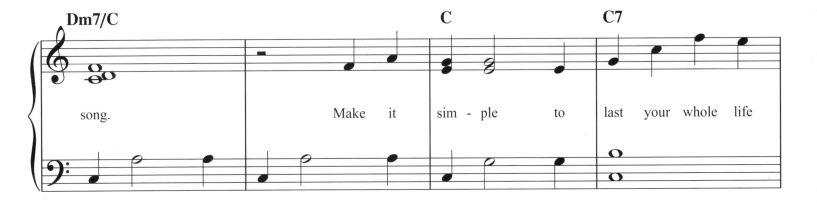

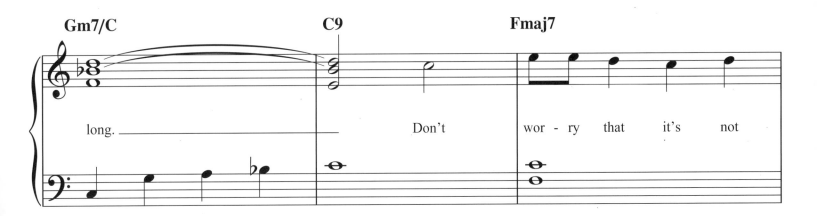

OVER THE RAINBOW
from THE WIZARD OF OZ

Music by HAROLD ARLEN
Lyric by E.Y. "YIP" HARBURG

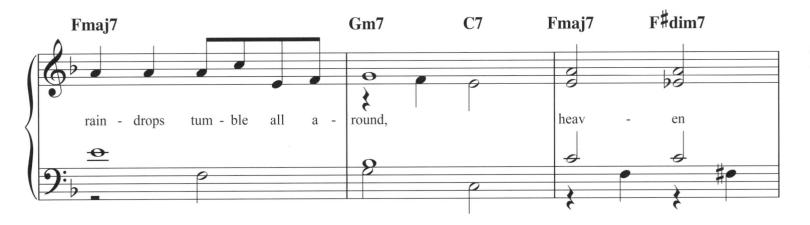

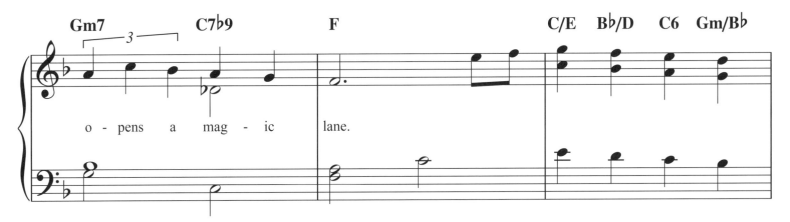

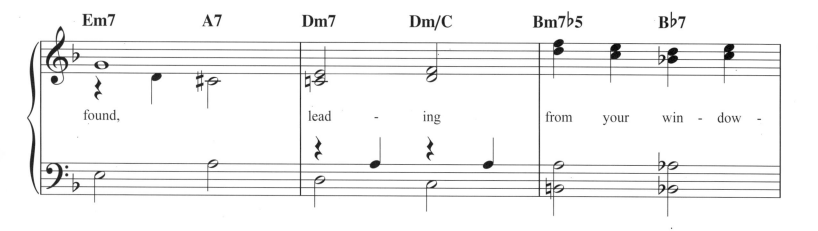

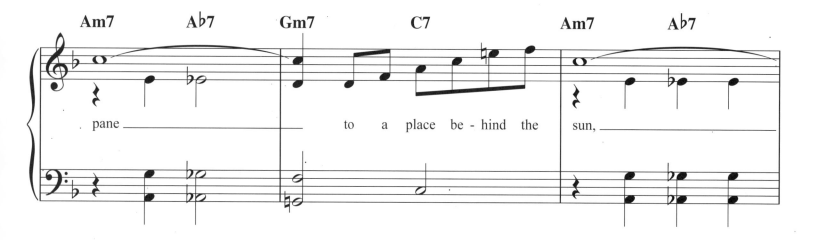

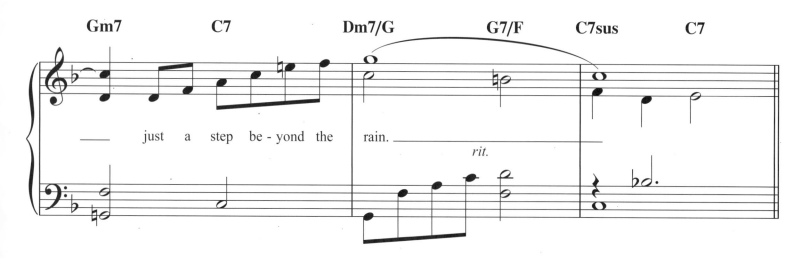

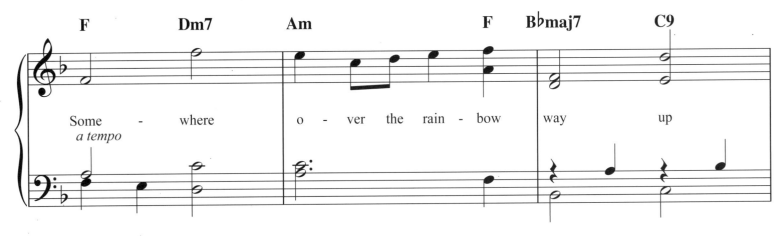

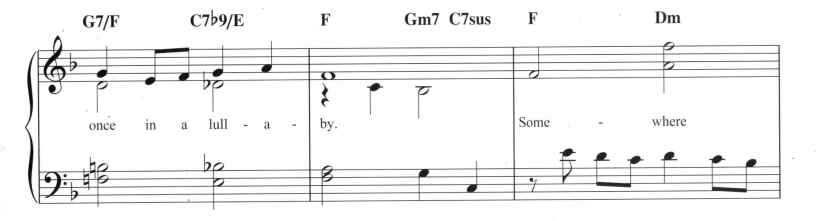

92

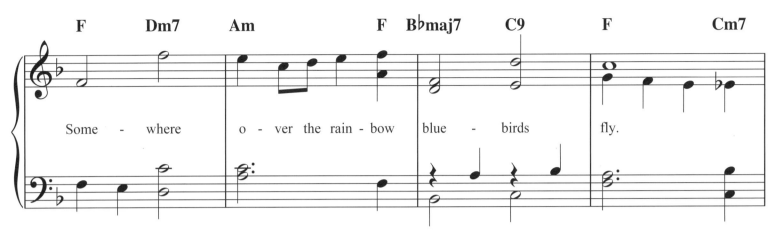

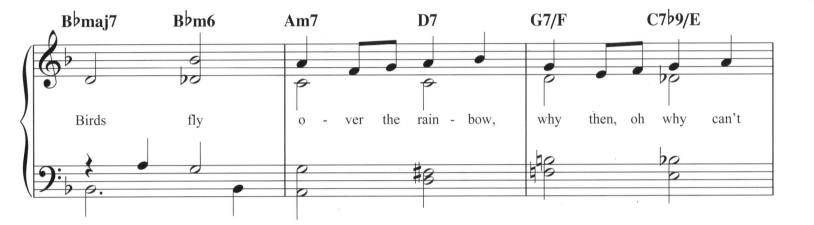

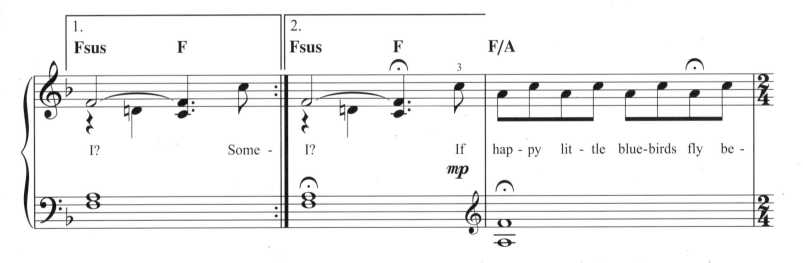

PUFF THE MAGIC DRAGON

Words and Music by LENNY LIPTON
and PETER YARROW

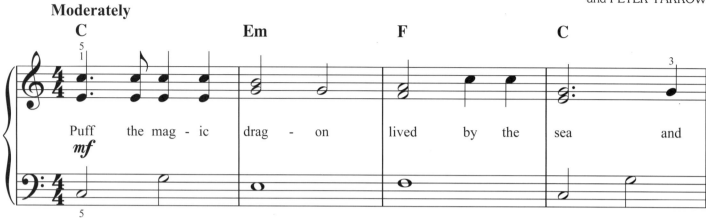

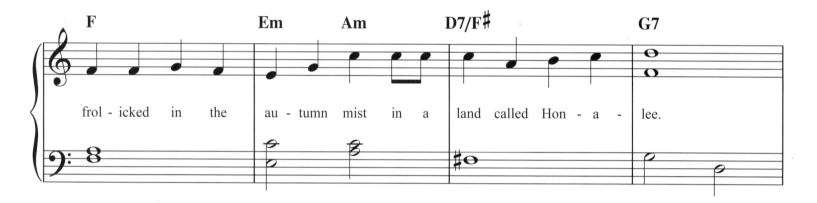

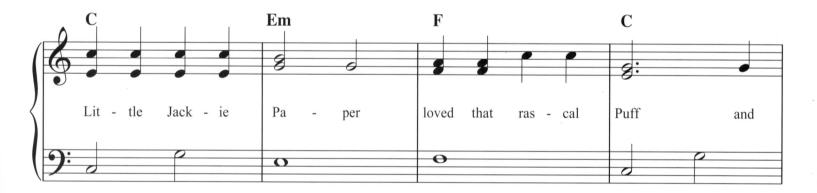

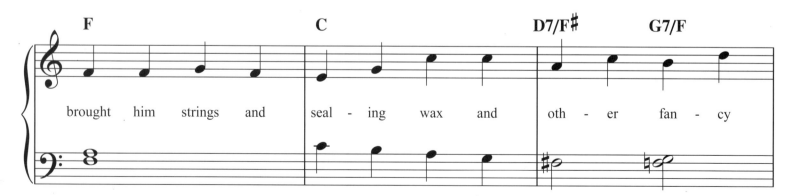

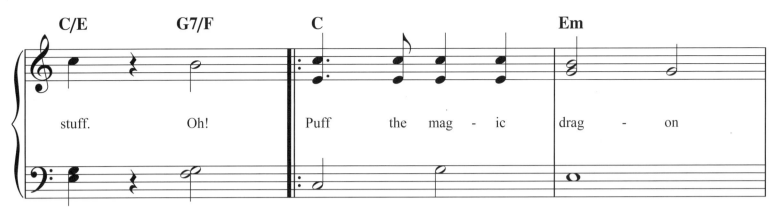
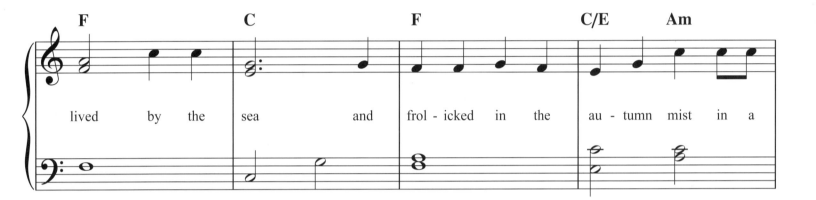
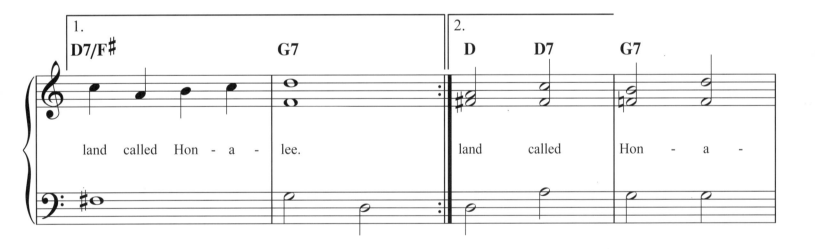
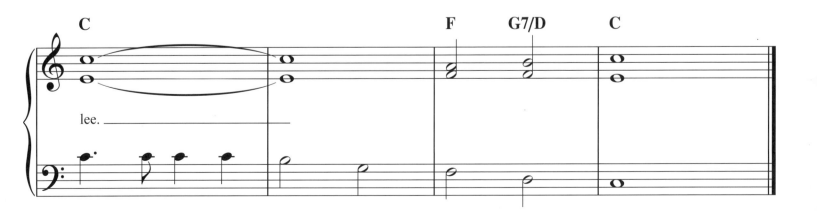

THE RAINBOW CONNECTION
from THE MUPPET MOVIE

Words and Music by PAUL WILLIAMS
and KENNETH L. ASCHER

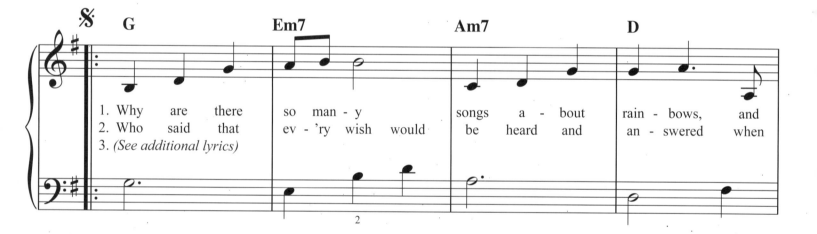

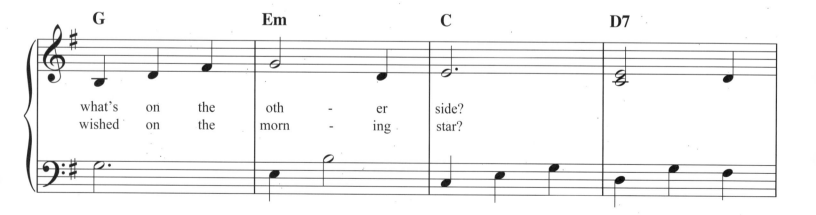

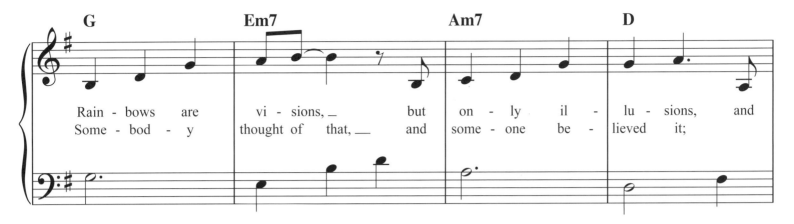

G **Em7** **Am7** **D**

Rain - bows are vi - sions, __ but on - ly il - lu - sions, and
Some - bod - y thought of that, __ and some - one be - lieved it;

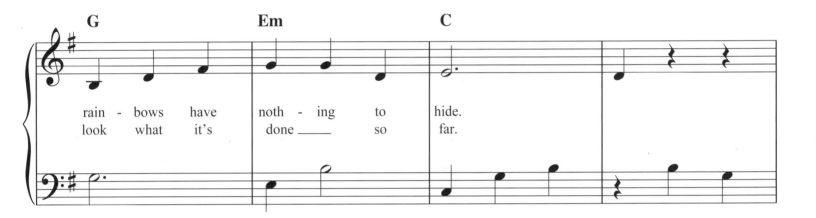

G **Em** **C**

rain - bows have noth - ing to hide.
look what it's done ___ so far.

Cmaj7 **Am7** **D**

So we've been told, and some choose to be - lieve it;
What's so a - maz - ing that keeps us star - gaz - ing and

Bm7

I know they're wrong; wait and see. ___
what do we think we might see? ___

Some - day we'll find it, the Rain - bow Con - nec - tion; the

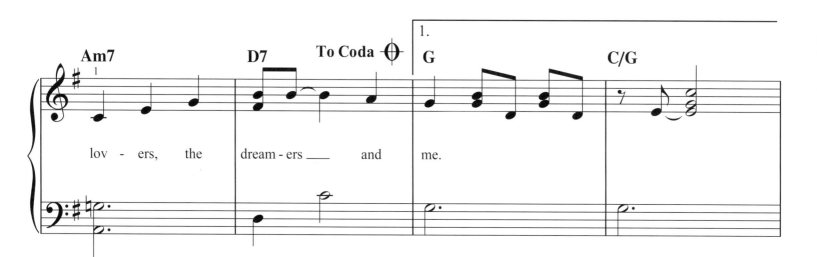

lov - ers, the dream - ers ___ and me.

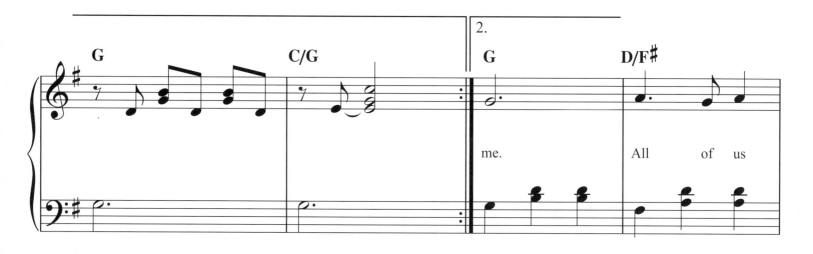

me. All of us

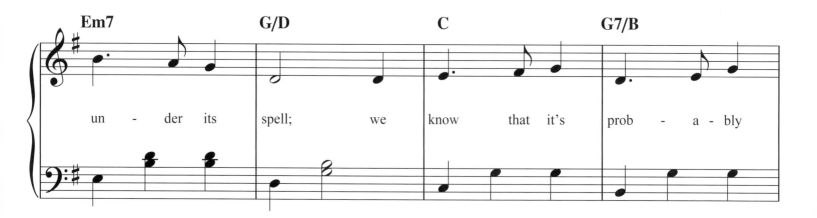

un - der its spell; we know that it's prob - a - bly

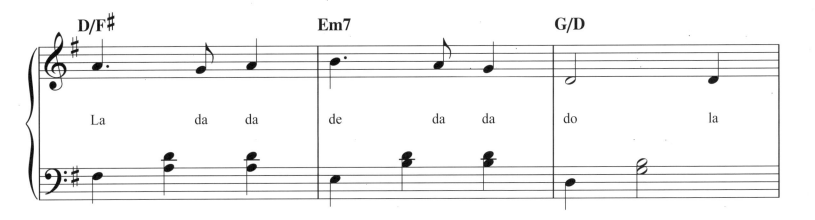

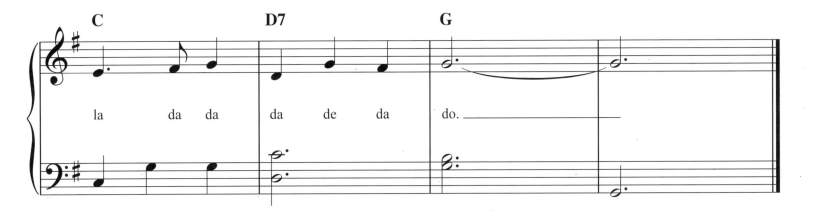

Additional Lyrics

3. Have you been half asleep and have you heard voices?
   I've heard them calling my name.
   Is this the sweet sound that calls the young sailors?
   The voice might be one and the same.
   I've heard it too many times to ignore it.
   It's something that I'm s'posed to be.
   Someday we'll find it,
   The Rainbow Connection;
   The lovers, the dreamers and me.

SESAME STREET THEME

Words by BRUCE HART,
JON STONE and JOE RAPOSO
Music by JOE RAPOSO

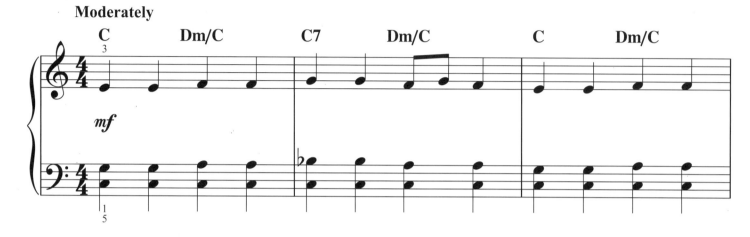

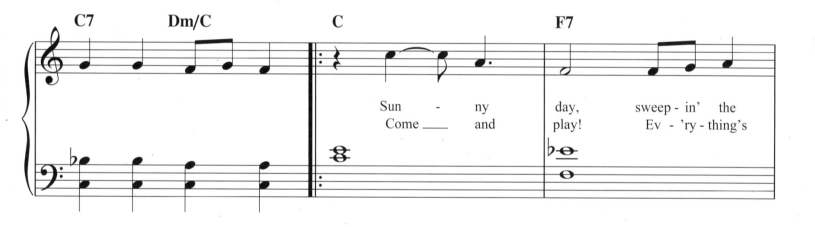

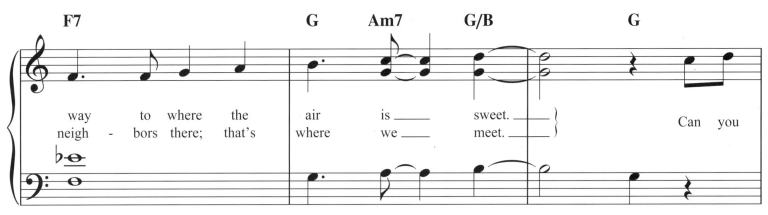

way   to   where   the   air   is ____   sweet. ____
neigh - bors   there; that's   where   we ____ meet. ____

Can you

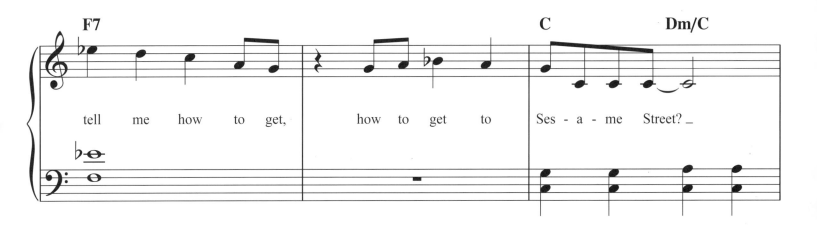

tell   me   how   to   get,   how   to   get   to   Ses - a - me   Street? _

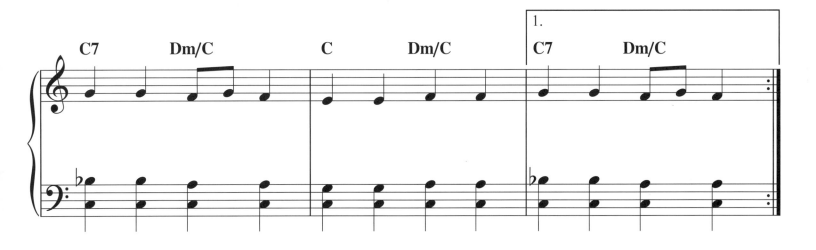

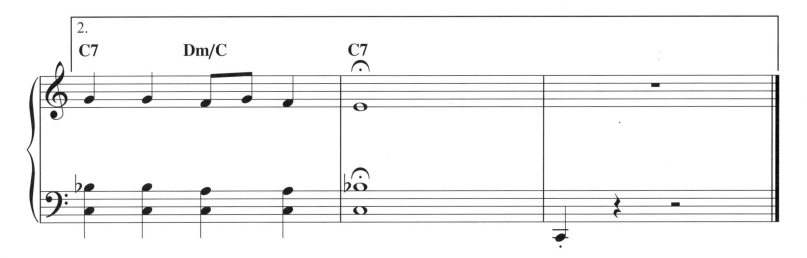

SKATING

By VINCE GUARALDI

Bright Jazz Waltz

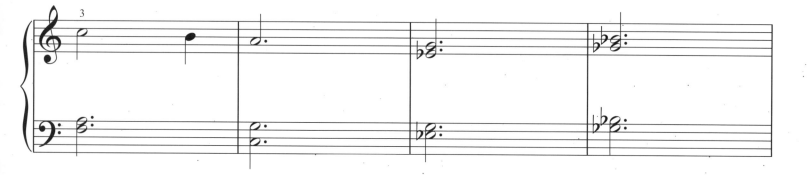

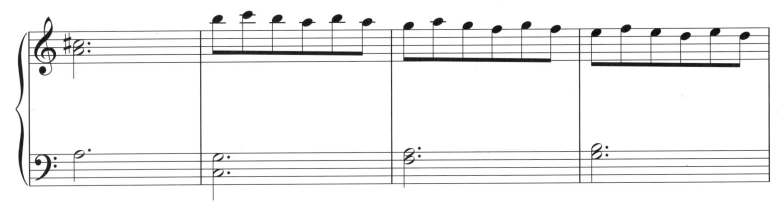

To Coda ⊕

1.

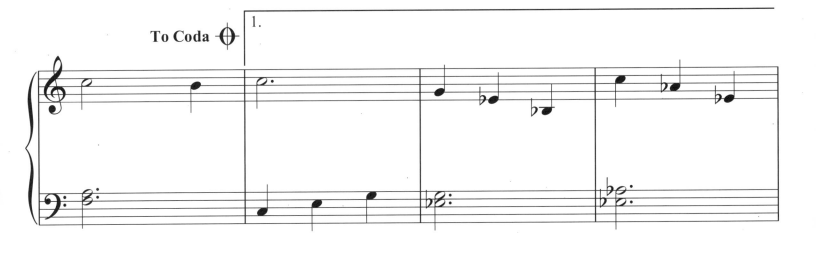

2.

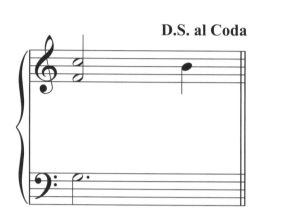

D.S. al Coda

CODA

SINGIN' IN THE RAIN

from SINGIN' IN THE RAIN

Lyric by ARTHUR FREED
Music by NACIO HERB BROWN

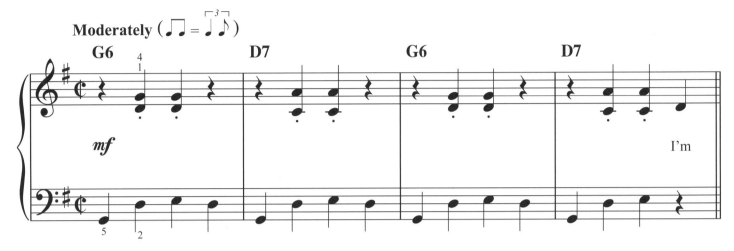

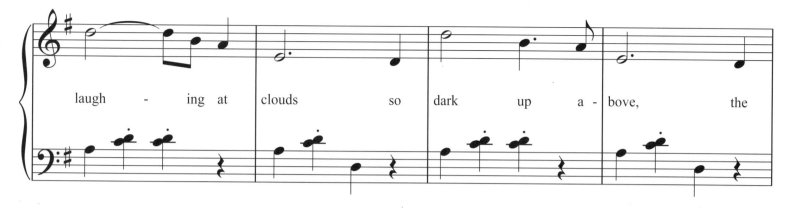

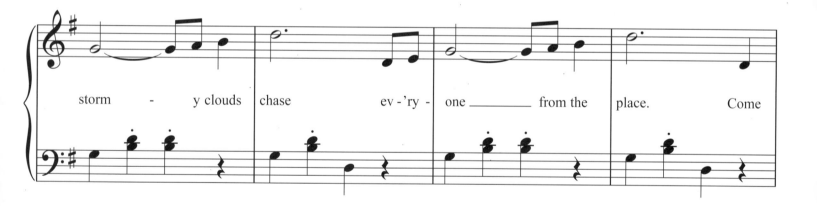

To Coda ⊕

walk down the lane with a hap - py re - frain, and

G6   **D7**

sing - in', _____ just sing - in' in _____ the rain.

E♭7   **G6**

Why am I smil - in' and why do I sing? _____

E♭7   **G6**

Why does De - cem - ber seem sun - ny as Spring? _____

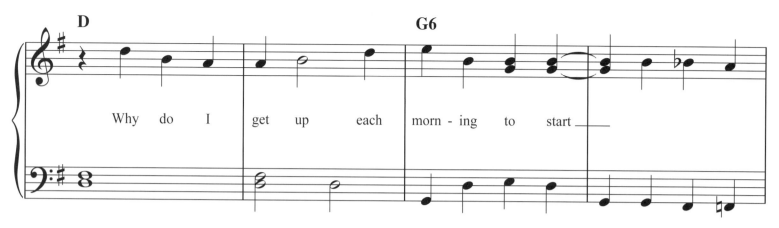

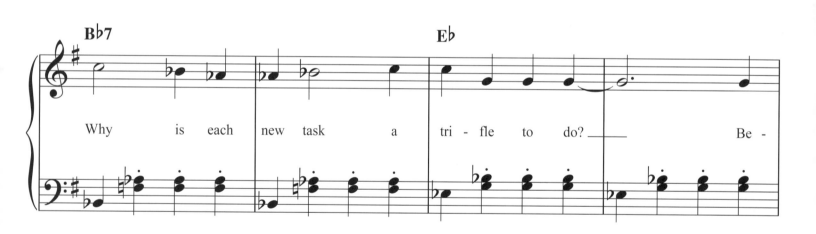

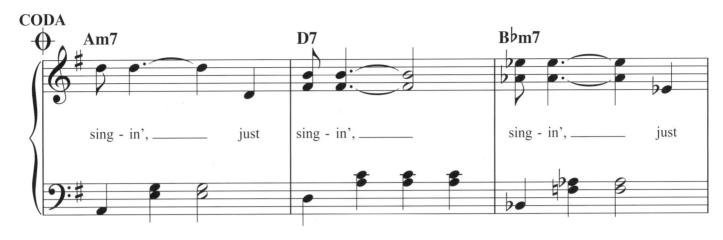

SPLISH SPLASH

Words and Music by BOBBY DARIN
and MURRAY KAUFMAN

Moderately, with a beat

Splish splash, I was   tak - in' a bath
Bing bang, ___ I   saw the whole gang,

'long a - bout - a Sat - ur - day   night.   A rub dub, just rel -
danc - in' on my liv - in' room rug.   Flip flop, they were

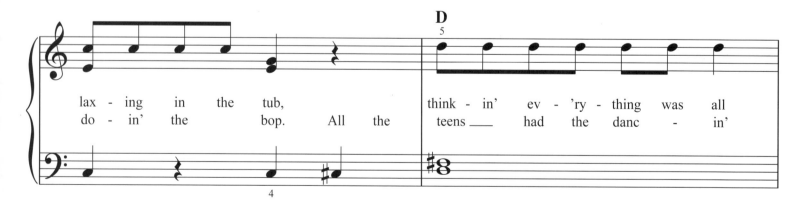

lax - ing in the tub,   think - in' ev - 'ry - thing was all
do - in' the bop. All the   teens ___ had the danc - in'

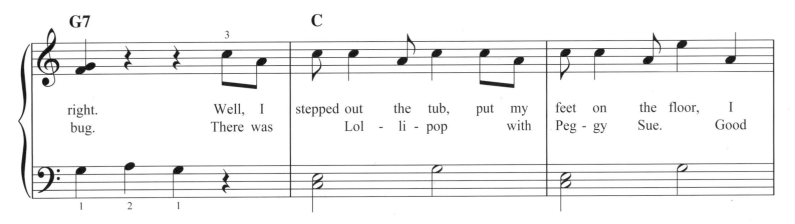

G7   **C**

right.
bug.

Well, I
There was

stepped out the tub, put my
Lol - li - pop with

feet on the floor, I
Peg - gy Sue. Good

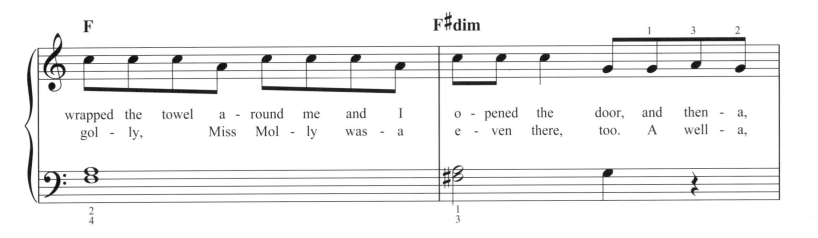

F   **F♯dim**

wrapped the towel a - round me and I
gol - ly, Miss Mol - ly was - a

o - pened the door, and then a,
e - ven there, too. A well - a,

C   **G7**

splish splash,
splish splash,

I
I for -

jumped back in the bath. ____
got a - bout the bath. ____

Well,
I

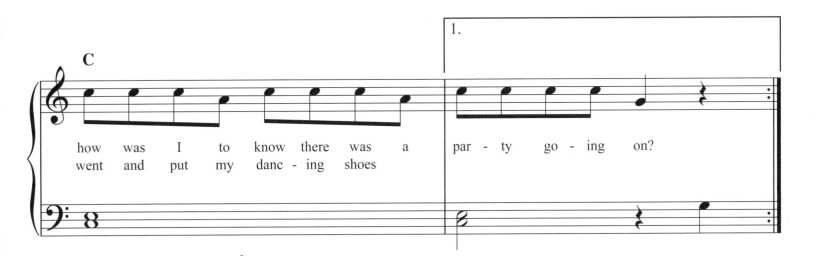

1.

C

how was I to know there was a
went and put my danc - ing shoes

par - ty go - ing on?

2.

on.   I   was   a -   splish - in'   and   a - splash - in'.

I   was   a -   roll - in'   and   a - stroll - in'.

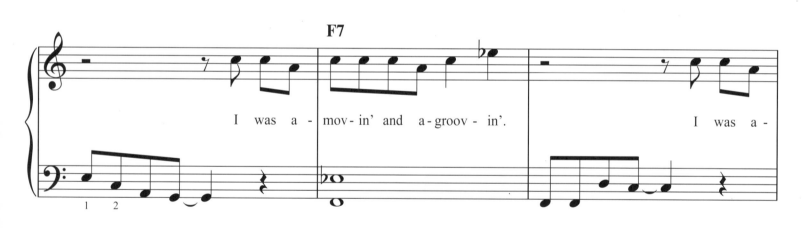

F7

I   was   a - mov - in'   and   a - groov - in'.   I   was   a -

C   **1.**   **2.**

reel - in'   with   the   feel - in'.   I   was   a -

SUPERCALIFRAGILISTIC-EXPIALIDOCIOUS

from MARY POPPINS

Words and Music by RICHARD M. SHERMAN
and ROBERT B. SHERMAN

Brightly

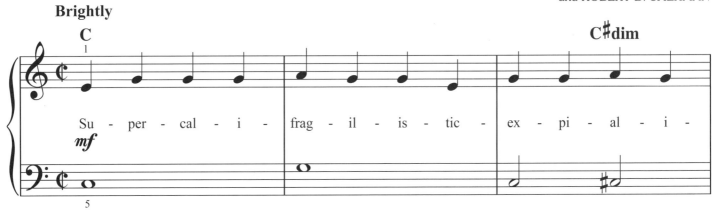

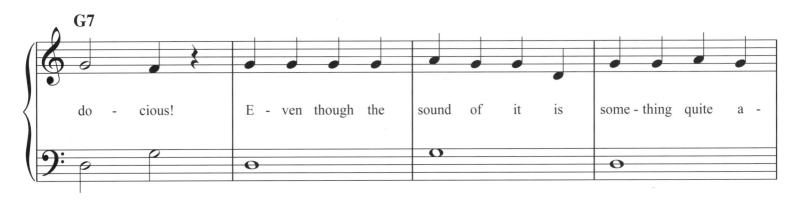

Su - per - cal - i - frag - il - is - tic - ex - pi - al - i - do - cious!

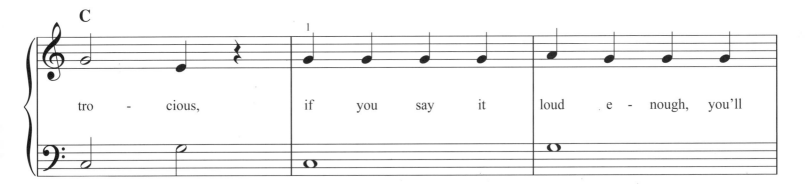

E - ven though the sound of it is some - thing quite a - tro - cious, if you say it loud e - nough, you'll

al - ways sound pre - co - cious. Su - per - cal - i - frag - il - is - tic -

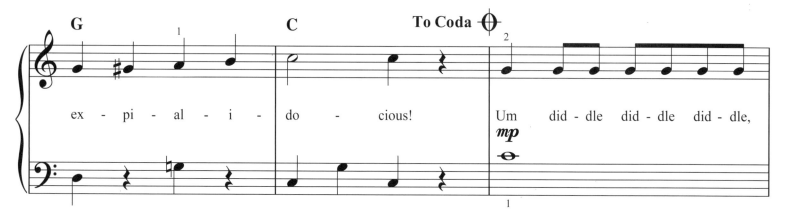

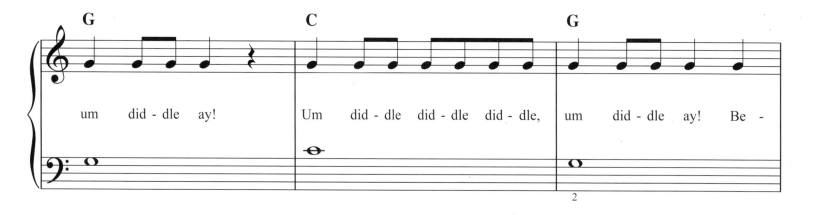

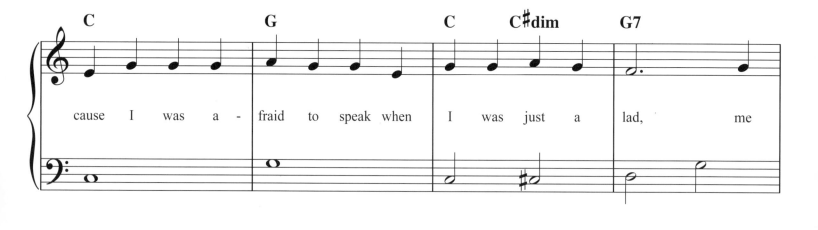

C

bad. But then one day I learned a word that

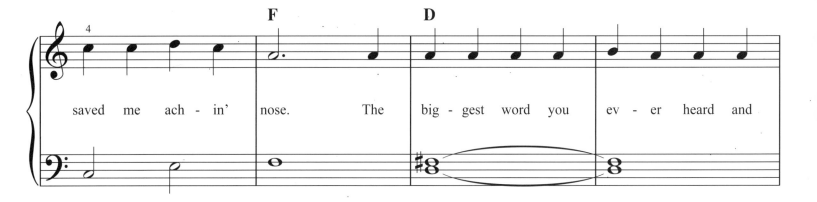

F   **D**

saved me ach - in' nose. The big - gest word you ev - er heard and

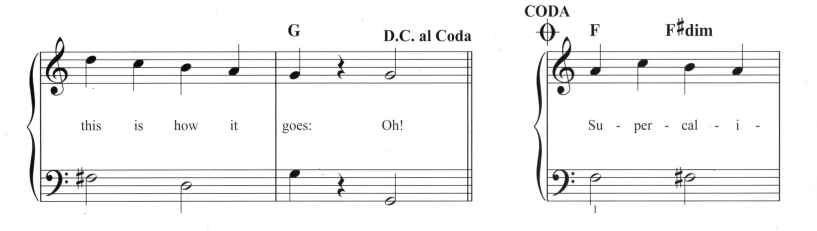

G   **D.C. al Coda**   **CODA**   **F**   **F♯dim**

this is how it goes: Oh!   Su - per - cal - i -

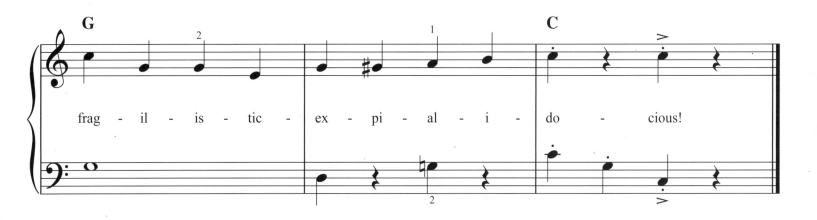

G   **C**

frag - il - is - tic - ex - pi - al - i - do - cious!

SPONGEBOB SQUAREPANTS THEME SONG

from SPONGEBOB SQUAREPANTS

Words and Music by MARK HARRISON,
BLAISE SMITH, STEVE HILLENBURG
and DEREK DRYMON

Moderately

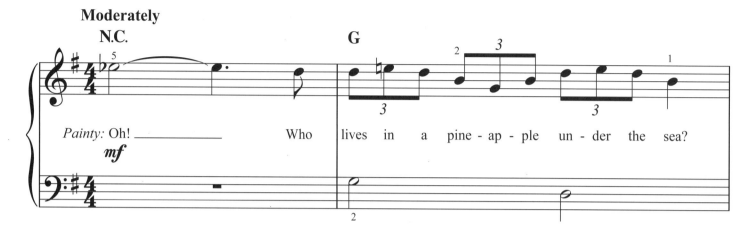

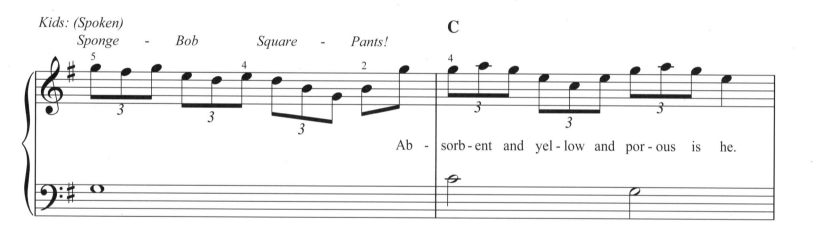

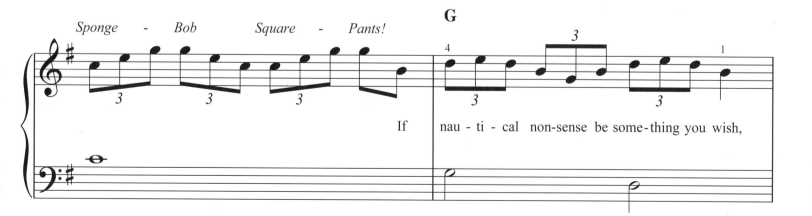

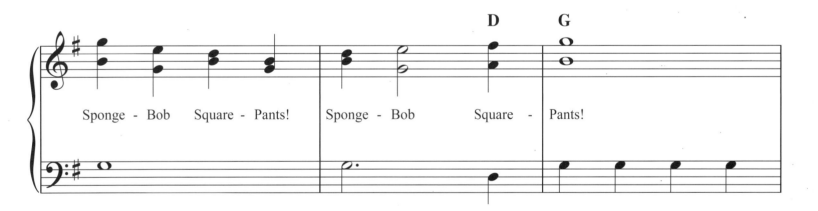

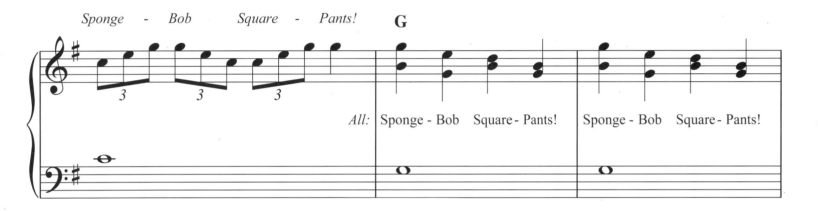

THE STAR SPANGLED BANNER

Words by FRANCIS SCOTT KEY
Music by JOHN STAFFORD SMITH

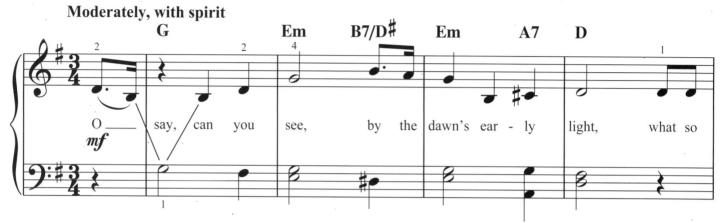

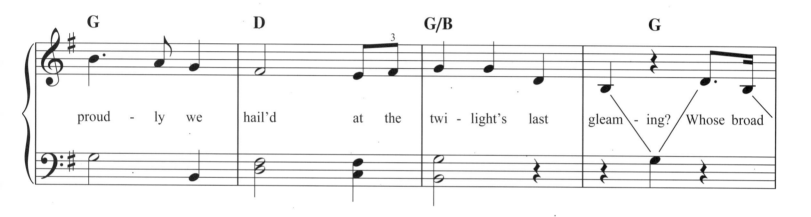

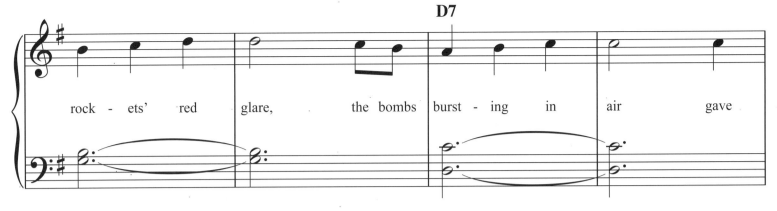

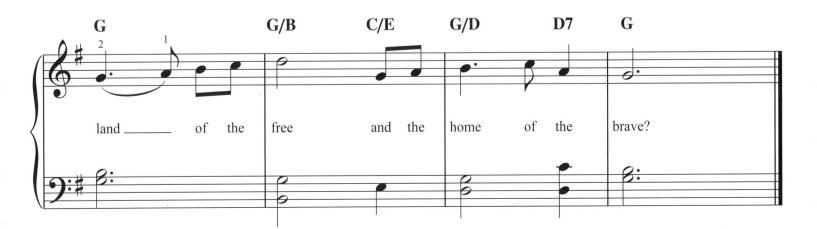

TAKE ME OUT TO THE BALL GAME

Words by JACK NORWORTH
Music by ALBERT VON TILZER

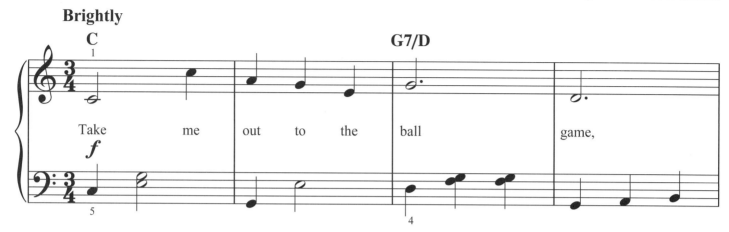

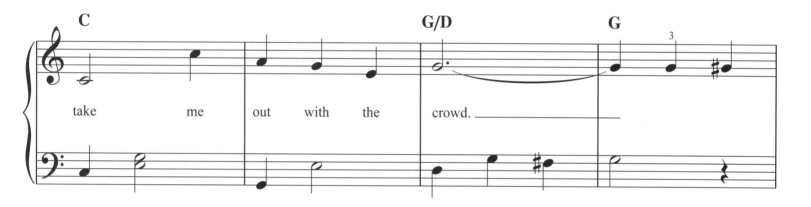

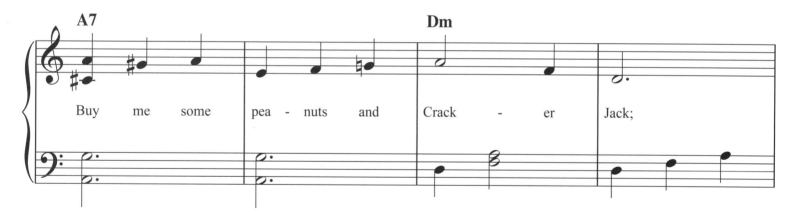

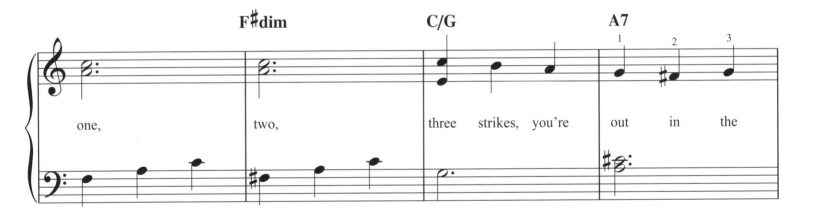

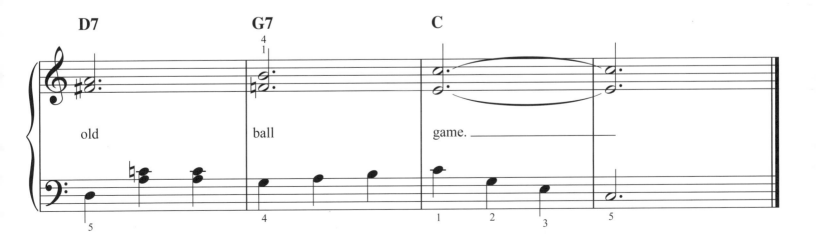

THIS LAND IS YOUR LAND

Words and Music by
WOODY GUTHRIE

With gusto

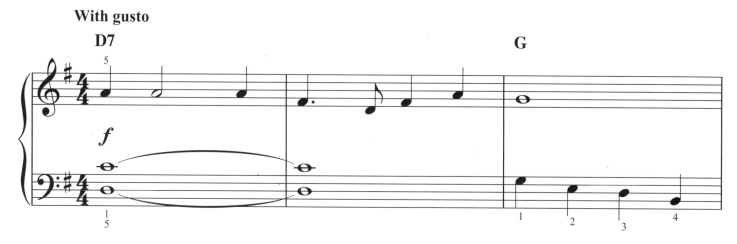

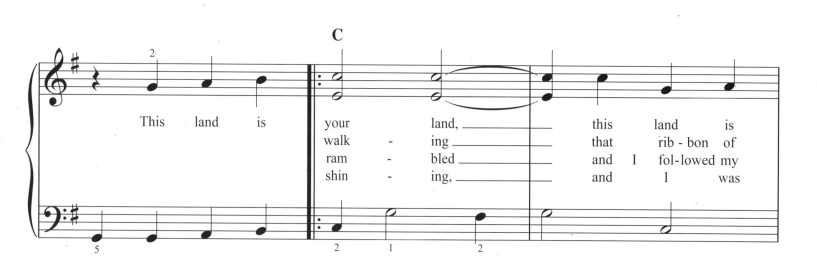

This land is your land, _____ this land is
walk - ing _____ that rib - bon of
ram - bled _____ and I fol-lowed my
shin - ing, _____ and I was

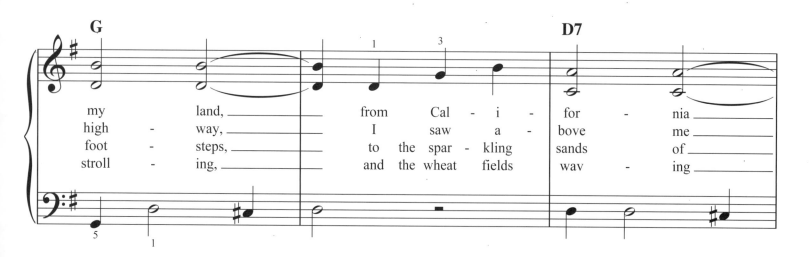

my land, _____ from Cal - i - for - nia _____
high - way, _____ I saw a - bove me _____
foot - steps, _____ to the spar - kling sands of _____
stroll - ing, _____ and the wheat fields wav - ing _____

123

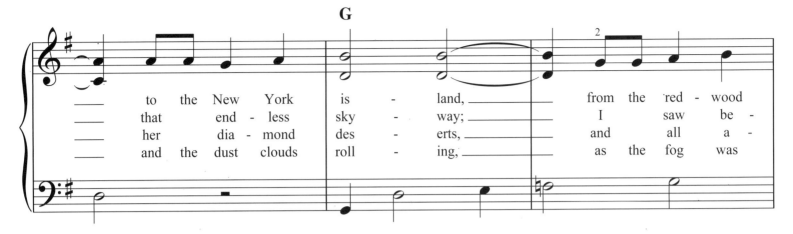

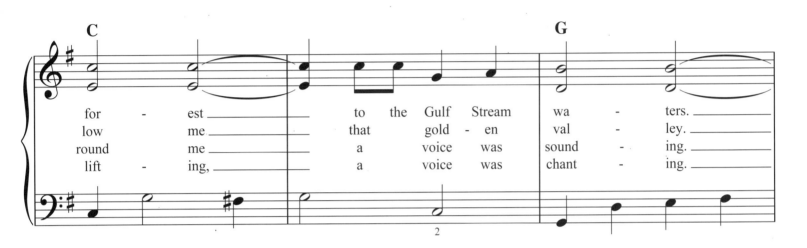

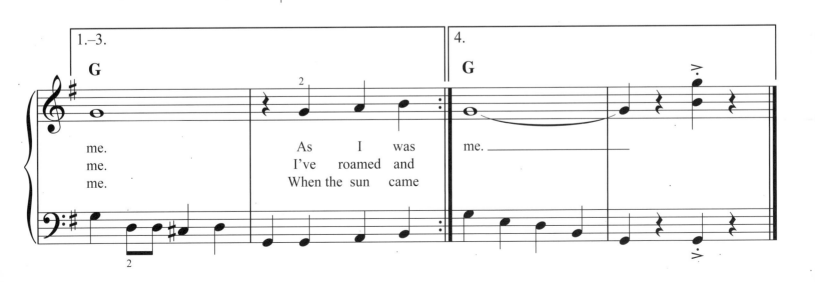

THIS OLD MAN

Traditional

This old man, he played one.

He played knick-knack on my drum, with a knick-knack pad-dy-whack,

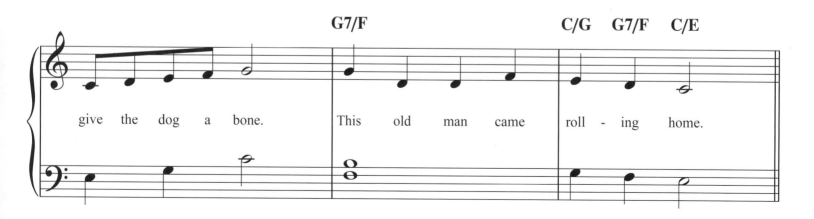

give the dog a bone. This old man came roll-ing home.

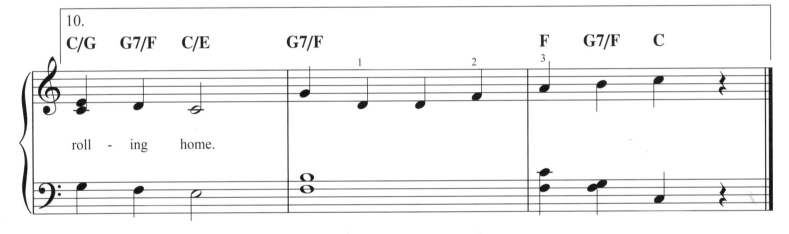

Additional Lyrics

3. This old man, he played three.
   He played knick-knack on my knee,
   Chorus

4. This old man, he played four.
   He played knick-knack on my door,
   Chorus

5. This old man, he played five.
   He played knick-knack on my hive,
   Chorus

6. This old man, he played six.
   He played knick-knack on my sticks,
   Chorus

7. This old man, he played seven.
   He played knick-knack up to heaven,
   Chorus

8. This old man, he played eight.
   He played knick-knack at the gate,
   Chorus

9. This old man, he played nine.
   He played knick-knack on my line,
   Chorus

10. This old man, he played ten.
    He played knick-knack over again,
    Chorus

THE UNICORN

Words and Music by
SHEL SILVERSTEIN

long time a-go when the earth was green, _ there were more kinds of an-i-mals than

you've ev - er seen. And they run a-round free while the world was be-ing born, and the

love - li - est of all was the u - ni - corn. There was green al - li - ga - tors and

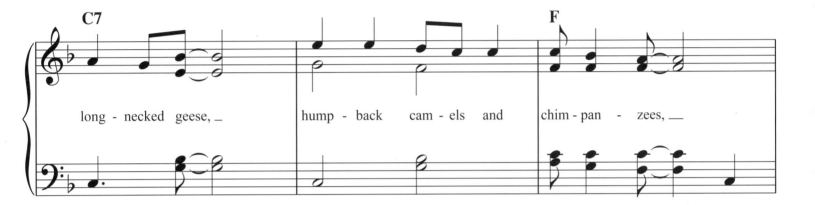

long - necked geese, _ hump - back cam - els and chim - pan - zees, _

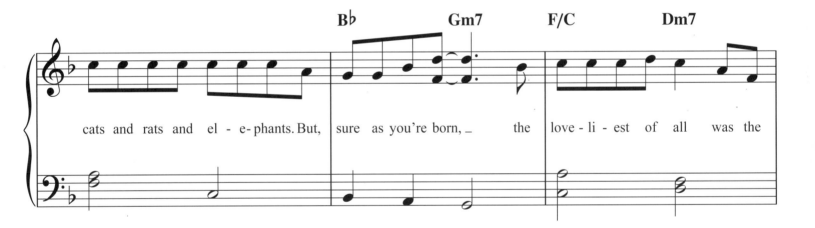

cats and rats and el - e - phants. But, sure as you're born, _ the love - li - est of all was the

u - ni - corn.

WHEN I GROW TOO OLD TO DREAM

Lyrics by OSCAR HAMMERSTEIN II
Music by SIGMUND ROMBERG

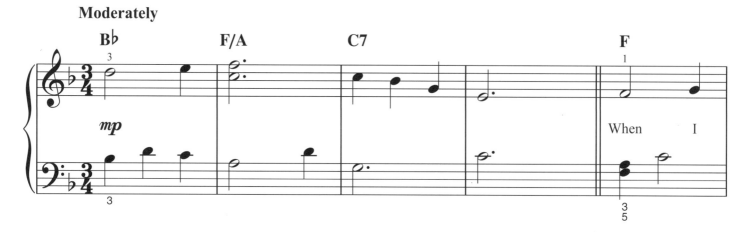

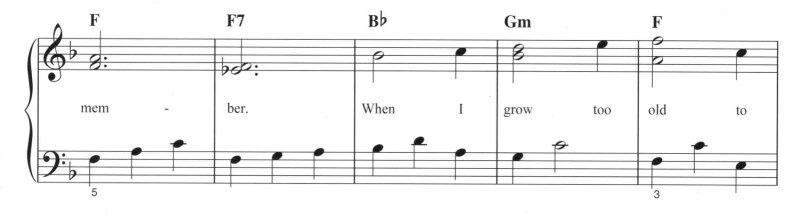

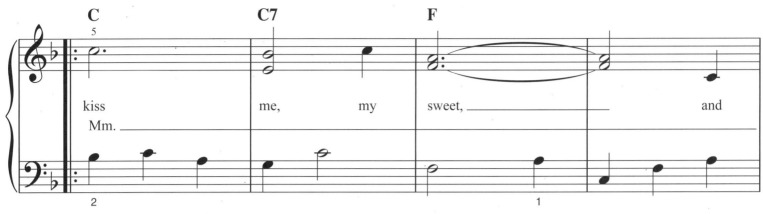

kiss me, my sweet, ___ and
Mm. ___

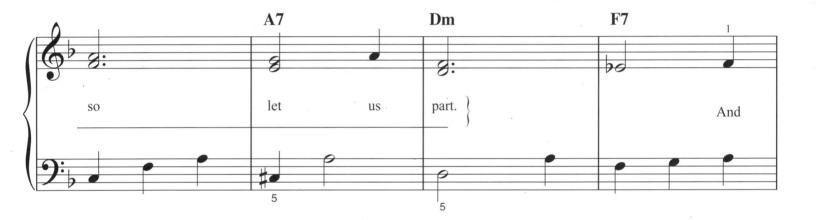

so let us part. And

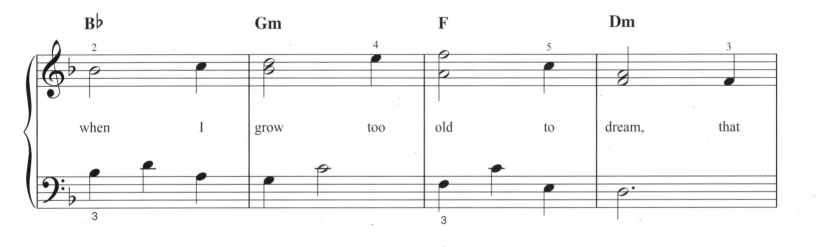

when I grow too old to dream, that

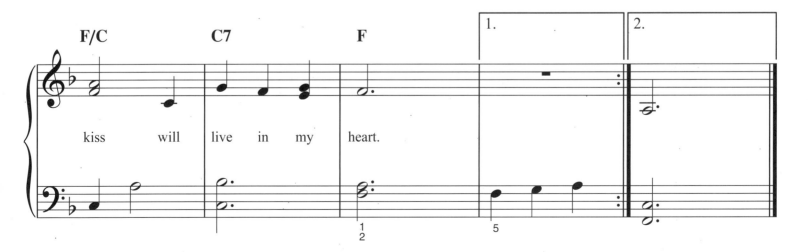

kiss will live in my heart.

WHEN YOU WISH UPON A STAR

from PINOCCHIO

Words by NED WASHINGTON
Music by LEIGH HARLINE

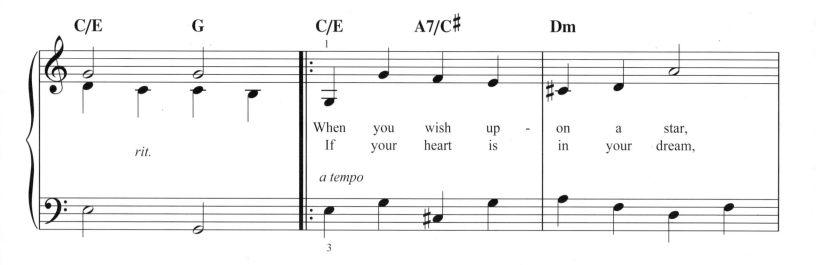

When you wish up - on a star,
If your heart is in your dream,

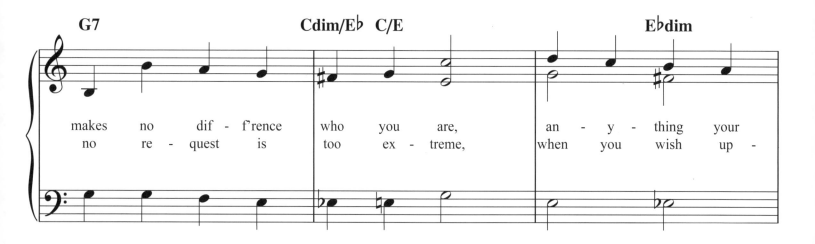

makes no dif - f'rence who you are, an - y - thing your
no re - quest is too ex - treme, when you wish up -

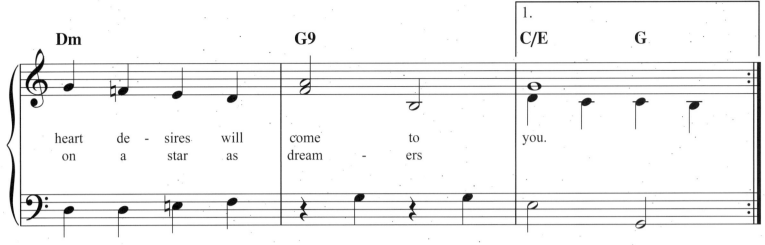

heart de - sires will come to you.
on a star as dream - ers

do. Fate is kind,

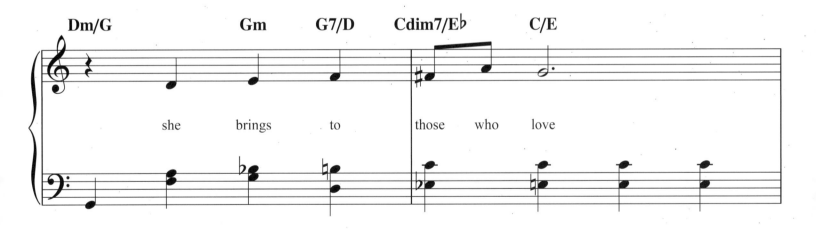

she brings to those who love

the sweet ful - fill - ment of their se - cret

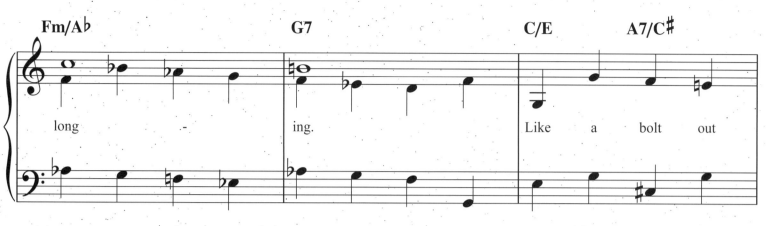

WHO'S AFRAID OF THE BIG BAD WOLF?

from THREE LITTLE PIGS

Words and Music by FRANK CHURCHILL
Additional Lyric by ANN RONELL

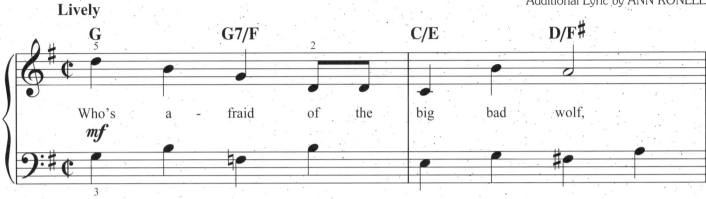

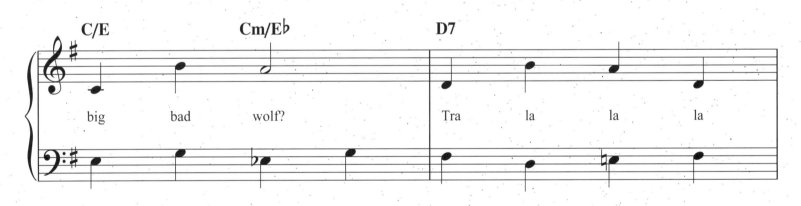

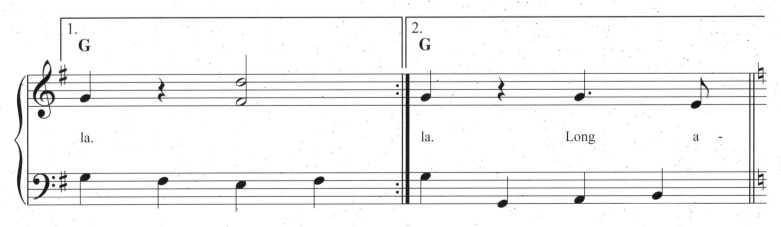

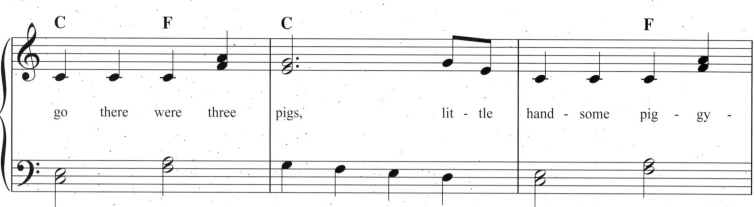

go there were three pigs, lit - tle hand - some pig - gy -

wigs. For the big bad, ver - y big ver - y bad __ wolf, they __

did - n't give three figs. Num - ber one was ver - y

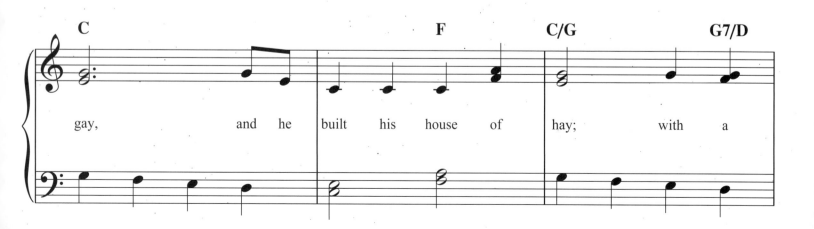

gay, and he built his house of hay; with a

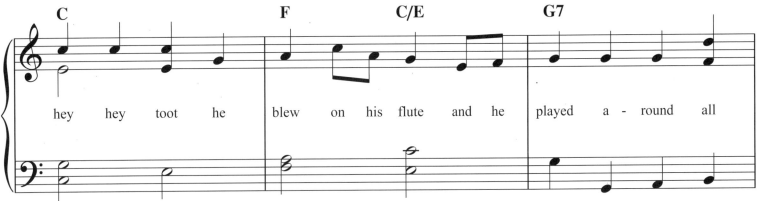

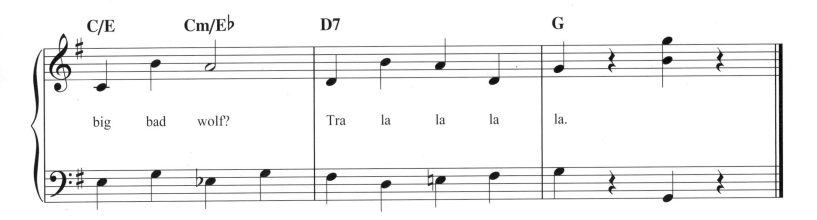

WON'T YOU BE MY NEIGHBOR?

(It's a Beautiful Day in the Neighborhood)
from MISTER ROGERS' NEIGHBORHOOD

Words and Music by
FRED ROGERS

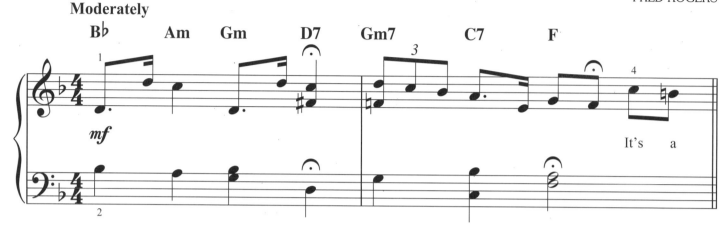

Moderately

It's a

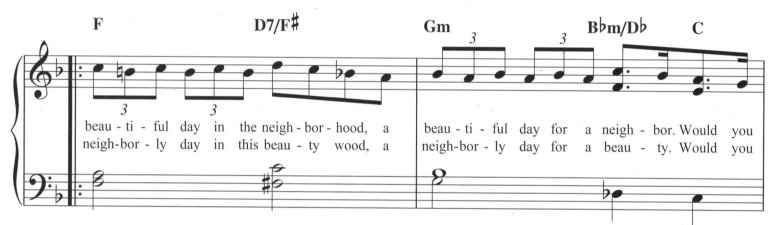

beau-ti-ful day in the neigh-bor-hood, a   beau-ti-ful day for a neigh-bor. Would you
neigh-bor-ly day in this beau-ty wood, a   neigh-bor-ly day for a beau-ty. Would you

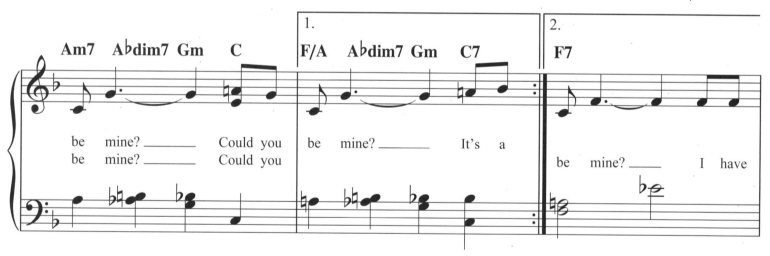

be mine? _____ Could you   be mine? _____ It's a
be mine? _____ Could you

1.

2.

be mine? _____ I have

al-ways want-ed to have a neigh-bor   just like you! _____ I've

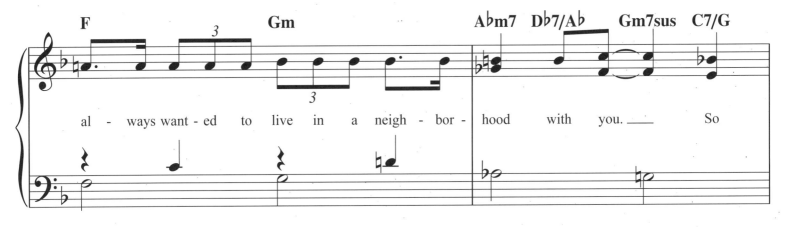

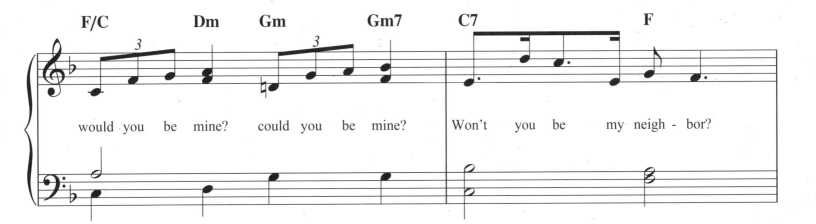

YANKEE DOODLE

Traditional

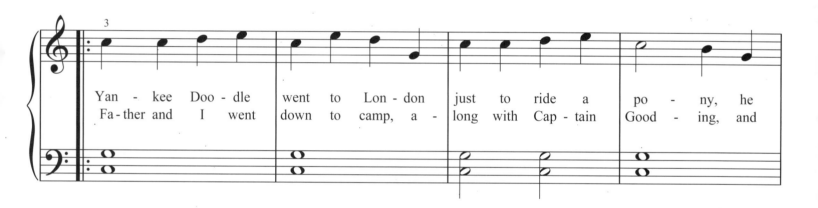

Yan - kee Doo - dle went to Lon - don just to ride a po - ny, he
Fa - ther and I went down to camp, a - long with Cap - tain Good - ing, and

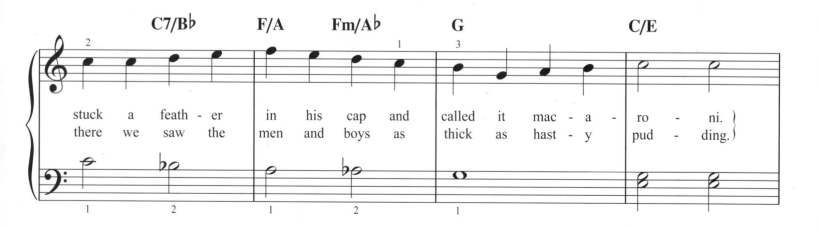

stuck a feath - er in his cap and called it mac - a - ro - ni.
there we saw the men and boys as thick as hast - y pud - ding.

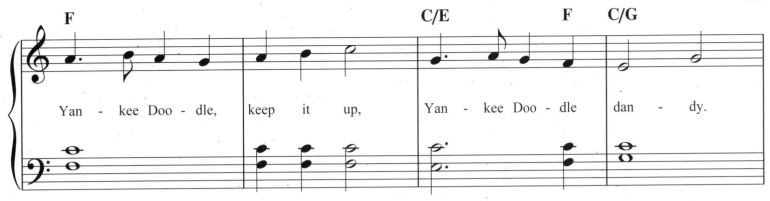

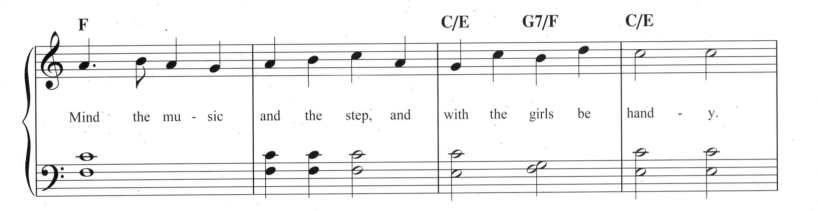

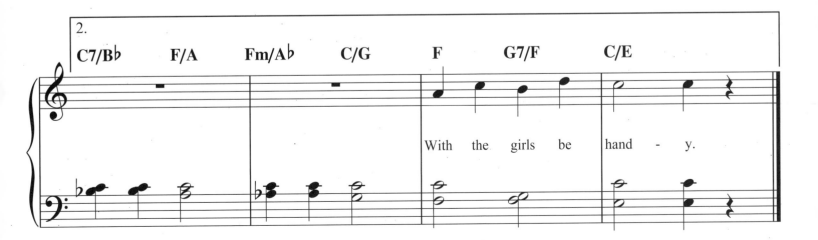

ZIP-A-DEE-DOO-DAH

from SONG OF THE SOUTH

Words by RAY GILBERT
Music by ALLIE WRUBEL

Zip - a-dee-doo - dah, zip - a-dee - ay!

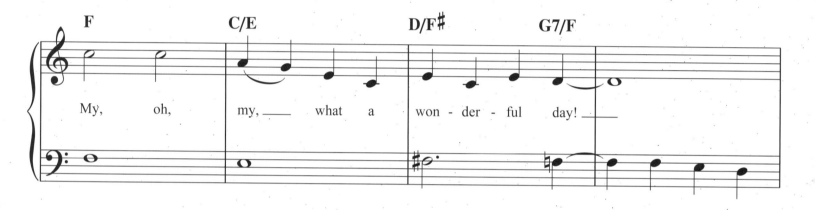

My, oh, my, _ what a won - der - ful day!

Plen - ty of sun - shine head - in' my way, _

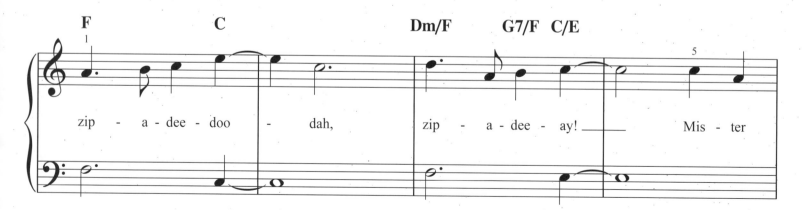

zip - a-dee-doo - dah, zip - a-dee - ay! _ Mis - ter

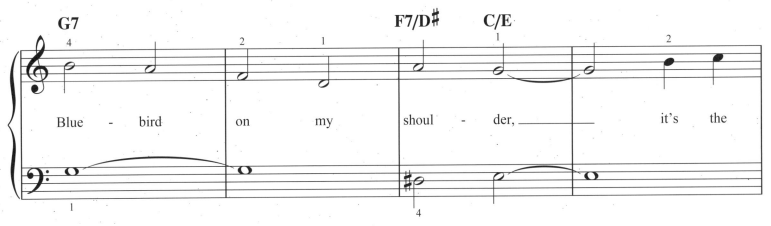

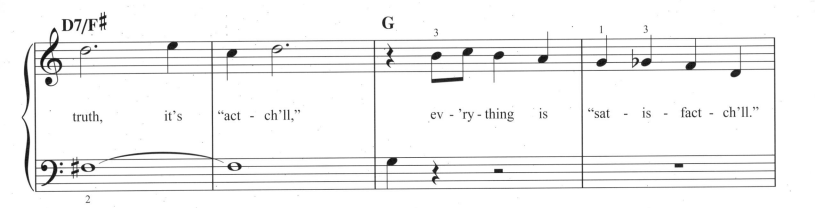

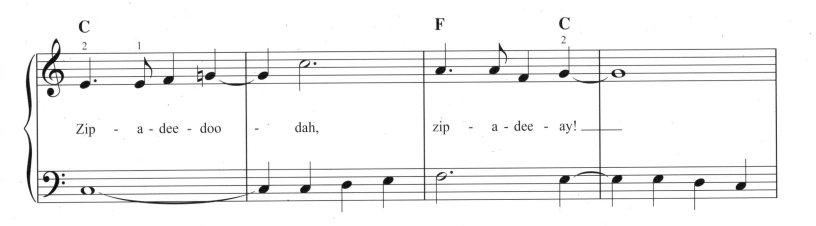

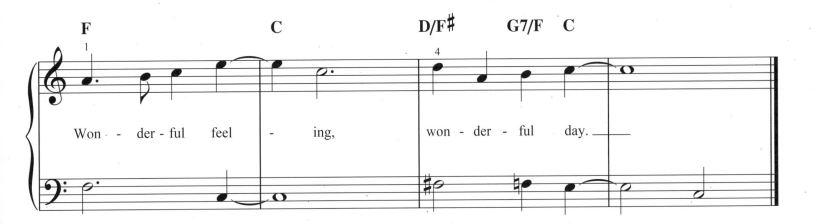

YOU ARE MY SUNSHINE

Words and Music by
JIMMIE DAVIS

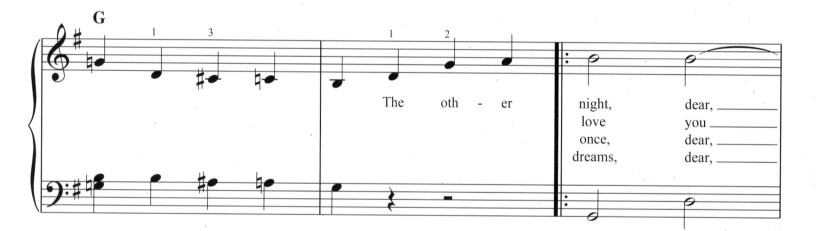

The oth - er | night, dear, _____
love you _____
once, dear, _____
dreams, dear, _____

_____ as I lay | sleep - ing _____ | I dreamed I | held you
and make you | hap - py _____ | if you will | on - ly
you real - ly | loved me _____ | and no | one could
you seem to | leave me. _____ | When I a - | wake my

in my arms,
say the same,
come be - tween,
poor heart pains.

but when I woke, dear, _____
but if you leave me _____
but now you've left me _____
So won't you come back

_____ I was mis - tak - en, _____
_____ and love an - oth - er, _____
_____ to love an - oth - er. _____
_____ and make me hap - py? _____

and I hung my _____
you'll re - gret it _____
You have shat - tered _____
I'll for - give, dear, I'll

head and I cried.
all some - day.
all of my dreams.
take all the blame.

You are my sun - shine, _____

_____ my on - ly sun - shine. _____ You make _ me hap - py when

skies   are   gray.   You'll nev - er   know,   dear, _____

_____ how much I   love _____ you. _____   Please don't take my

sun - shine a - way.

1.-3.
I'll   al - ways
You told me
In   all   my

4.